PHANTOM BLACK DOGS

WALKERS OF THE LIMINAL WAY

W.T. WATSON

BEYOND THE FRAY
Publishing

ISBN 13: 978-1-954528-12-3

Cover design: Disgruntled Dystopian Publications

Beyond The Fray Publishing, San Diego, CA
www.beyondthefraypublishing.com

BEYOND THE FRAY

Publishing

To Folklorists, past and present, and all the Fortean researchers who have sparked ideas found in these pages. Many thanks for all your hard work and keep digging!

INTRODUCTION

Eliminate all other factors, and the one which
remains must be the truth... "

Arthur Conan Doyle
The Sign of Four

———

The purpose of this book is to provide the reader with a brief
overview of the Phantom Black Dog phenomenon, an apparition that has taken its place in the history of the United Kingdom, the Americas and Europe. The lore of the Phantom Black
Dog is extensive and ranges from stories told in the 1500s and
earlier to the modern day. That lore includes many regional
legends, witness accounts collected by folklorists and others, as
well as newspaper articles and modern-day website databases of
sightings.

It is my purpose to write an informal introduction to this
wonderful and interesting aspect of high strangeness. As such, I
will eschew the conventions of formal writing and will stick to a

more conversational style. I've found that this approach helps keep the text from sounding like someone's doctoral thesis rather than a book designed to inform and, hopefully, entertain.

In line with that determination, I am going to cite sources in the text of the book rather than distracting the reader with constant footnotes. At the end of the book, you will find a reasonably extensive bibliography that will provide you with books, articles, websites and even a television episode or two related to this phenomenon and related items of interest that I talk about throughout the book.

Before launching into the fascinating world of the Phantom Black Dog, let me take a moment to introduce myself.

I am a writer of both fiction and non-fiction, and I love to infuse my work with my expertise in cryptozoology, monster lore, magic, Forteana and the paranormal. While no person can truly know everything there is to know about these topics, I come at this book with a thirty-plus-year obsession with things that go bump in the night.

My personal spiritual philosophy is grounded in animism, a topic I will take up later, and I am well versed in such topics as Harner-style shamanism and the occult. As such, I approach my topic from the animistic viewpoint that I mentioned above, and my thoughts on the Black Dog phenomenon stray heavily into occult territory.

The scientific method is a terrific way to examine some realities in our world, and the technology it breeds makes this book possible, so I am certainly not going to ignore science and tech, but I will say, from the outset, that the scientific method is extremely limited and limiting when it comes to exploration of Phantom Black Dogs or any other paranormal or Fortean topic.

The Phantom Black Dog is a particular subject of interest to me since my novel *Hunting The Beast*, and its sister stories that I hope to publish soon, uses the lore of the Black Dog as a jumping-off point into my fantasy world.

During my research for that book, I read many of the articles and books that you will find in the reference section, and I remember thinking, at the time, that this information would make a terrific book. When Beyond the Fray Publishing asked me to consider a non-fiction work on this subject, I could not resist the opportunity to bring this monster to the page. Please note that when I use the word monster here, I am harking back to the Latin *monstrum*, which referred to a divine omen (often a bad one) or portent and not necessarily the horror definition of a monster, which usually refers to something terrible that will eat you.

I have lived with a black dog (not of the Phantom sort) and have seen how differently people react to such a canine. My black dog was a fifty-pound Labrador/Border collie mix that my spouse and I acquired at the Buffalo, New York, pound. This active puppy received the name Echo since we intended to work with her in wilderness search and rescue, and we already had dogs named Sonar and Radar on the team.

Our new bundle of energy definitely needed a job, and over time, we trained with her in search and rescue, obedience and agility. Echo was smart and friendly, but, while most people had no issue with her, I noted that, occasionally, people would turn and walk away at the sight of her.

The most extreme example of this was a neighbour I had in an apartment complex in Alpharetta, Georgia, who would encounter us in the hallway as I took Echo out for potty time, and flee back into her apartment, locking the door behind her.

I came to find out, after doing some research, that in this person's culture, the djinn took the form of black dogs. Djinn are a type of Middle Eastern spirit that we will touch on later, and in

Islamic culture, they are to be avoided at all costs if one wishes to remain free of obsession, bad luck or worse.

I respected my neighbour's wishes and would pull Echo back into our apartment if she happened to be in the hallway, even though I was fairly certain that my dog was not a mischievous or evil spirit.

Our journey into the fascinating world of the Black Dog is going to cover a lot of ground. We will discuss what a Phantom Black Dog is, and we will look at locations where Black Dogs are seen most often. This perusal will even "cross the pond" and document some cases from the United States, Canada and Latin America, which we will define as the Hispanic countries south of the United States border.

We will speak extensively about the traits, both common and uncommon, of Black Dog sightings. We will also look at the in-depth coverage of the Black Dog by folklorists in Britain and some of the stories that they relay to us as well as more modern-day witness statements. To conclude, I will cover some of the theories that surround these shaggy beasts, ranging from the mundane to the outrageously esoteric.

I should also note that, due to space restrictions, there are several possible aspects of this phenomenon that I will not discuss in the book.

First, there are all manner of legends about the Phantom Black Dog. The legendary accounts can be found in the work of the folklorists who are cited in the bibliography, for those readers interested in pursuing the subject further. For the most part, unless I am dealing with a classic story like the Black Dog of Bungay or using a legend as background for a sighting, I will try to avoid these legends and stick to tales that come to us from witnesses. Given that many of these stories are taken by folklorists, the accounts may not be extensive, but I feel that getting the story from a witness adds to the interest of the book. Please note that some of the witnesses quoted come to us from folklore articles that try to capture the accent of the speaker. Also, some of these articles were written in the early twentieth century, so the language may seem archaic.

Another legend that I will not chase is the various myths of the Wild Hunt and their derivations. While it is true that all the Wild Huntsmen (and women, for that matter) are said to ride with hounds of one sort or the other, this mythic sequence has far more to do with ancient, pre-Christian religious ideas and less to do with our canine apparition. While our subject may be fierce, he does not, usually, seem willing to pluck one off the face of the earth and haul one off to the Underworld.

Before we begin our deep dive into the world of the Phantom Black Dog, I would like to present a tale that may be an urban legend, but which illustrates the type of story that we will hear over and over again in these pages. The story comes to us courtesy of the outstanding paranormalist, Lon Strickler and his *Phantoms and Monsters* blog, when two young men, driving in their car late at night, as young people are wont to do, suddenly have their night take a turn to the supernatural.

These two fellows, in North Carolina, USA, pass a church on Highway 194 in the interestingly named town of Valle Crucis (Valley of the Cross, in Latin). One explanation for the name of the town is that two creeks intersect in a perfect cross at that location. We will hear more about Black Dogs and water in the body of the book.

In any event, a shadow leaps out from behind one of the many gravestones in the church cemetery. The driver takes evasive action and misses the figure in the road, but when he stops to see what it is that he nearly hit, he sees a dog.

Not just any dog, mind you. The creature is as tall and wide as a man, with bristly black fur and eyes that glow a sullen, hellish red.

The two young men, not being feeble-minded, accelerate away from the scene only to have this massive dog give chase. They far exceed the speed limit in an effort to escape but are only able to shake their pursuer when they cross a bridge over running water. The tale ends in the town of Boone, North Carolina, with both young men sitting in a diner, eager for human company and knowing that they will not sleep that night.

This wonderful tale, which, as I mentioned, may be an urban (or, in this case, rural) legend is backed up by other witness testimony that we will discuss later. The story is a good jumping-off point for exploring the Phantom Black Dog legend. It is of modern provenance, but it mirrors tales that have been told in England and elsewhere for literal centuries.

Note these items in the tale as we go forward. A massive black dog. Shaggy fur. Glowing eyes. Pursuit through a specific course and then vanishing at a very specific border. We will see all these details and more as we delve into the world of the Phantom Black Dog.

Let's begin by defining just what it is that we are talking about.

SECTION ONE

WHAT IS A PHANTOM BLACK DOG?

The Black Dog has perhaps more vitality, and
survives in more localities, than all the
apparitions that in olden times were sworn to
by persons of the highest veracity. They may
still be heard of in many a nook and corner...

Richard Jeffries
Wild Life in a Southern County, as quoted by Theo Brown in *The
Black Dog*

1

BASIC DEFINITIONS

A PERSON HEARING the words "Phantom Black Dog" for the first time will usually have one of two reactions. They may either wonder what the speaker is talking about, or, if they are conversant with the lore of the British Isles or some American or European folk tales, their mind may wander back to the folklorists of the 1930s and 1950s who spent considerable time and effort documenting this then-famous apparition. As will be discovered in the course of the text, the Black Dog has a much wider habitat than just England, but it is the English folklorists and their extensive documentation that sets the stage for research into this arcane creature.

Those folklorists are quite adamant about one thing: witness veracity. Witnesses will be discussed in a later chapter of the book, but suffice to say that folklorists like Ethel Rudkin, whose seminal work started me down the Black Dog rabbit hole, are keen to show that the people they talked to were weak in neither mind nor body. As you peruse the many tales of the Black Dog, you discover that the witnesses are often country folk who would seem to have neither time nor motivation for making up stories.

In my mind, witnesses are the most important part of the phenomenon. Since sightings of Black Dogs and other apparitions are not repeatable incidents that will submit to the scientific method, the only source of information about these beings is the perceptions of the people who see the Black Dog and take the time to report it.

There is no need to take apart every witness statement and try to debunk it. It should go without saying that some witness statements have more of the ring of truth than others, and we should even assume that some witnesses will lie or hoax. Skepticism, that is the practice of actually having one's mind open to all possibilities, mundane and esoteric, is the proper state of mind for approaching a witness.

When you begin to examine the Black Dog lore, you find a mass of people – ordinary people, like you and me – who have seen something they felt was extraordinary. This fact should be enough to take any person with an open mind into an examination of what witnesses have to say and to follow where those stories lead. As will be seen in these pages, those tales took me into places I could not have imagined over the course of the research.

So, for those not familiar with the subject, some basics on the Phantom Black Dog will help make this text more understandable.

NAMES

One of the things discovered in the research is that this creature goes by many local names. Some people will refer to the Black Dog as a hellhound, an understandable moniker considering our subject's often frightening appearance. I will take up my reasons for saying that hellhound is a misnomer in a later part of the book.

Other Black Dogs take their names from the area where they are most often seen, such as the Black Dog of the Hanging Hills, whom we will meet in the section on death portents. M. V. Dahlgren tells us of a Maryland, USA, variant of the Black Dog called Snarly Yow, a wonderfully onomatopoeic name.

The people of the British Isles have given the anomalous creature numerous names throughout the many provinces of that country. According to Kiersten Carr in her master's thesis "Hellhounds and Helpful Ghost Dogs", the Black Dog is called "the Gwyllgi in Wales, Black Shuck in East Anglia, Yeth hound or Wishthounds in Devonshire, Skriker in Lancashire, Barguest or Gytrash in Yorkshire, Padfoot in West Yorkshire, Hairy Jack in Lincolnshire, the Moddey Dhoo on the Isle of Man, the Gurt Dog in Somerset, the Muckle Black Tyke in Scotland, and the Grim", amongst many other names.

Bob Trubshaw gives the following names for the Black Dog in English folklore: Gurt Dog, Old Shuck or Shock, Devil's Dandy (or Dando) Dogs, Yeth (Heath) or Wisht Hound, Barguest, Black Shag, Padfoot, Hooter, Guytrash, Skriker, Moddey Dhoo, Matthew Doog and possibly the Pooka.

From personal knowledge of faery lore, I would take issue with the Pooka title. The Pooka is a shape-shifting fae that may take the form of a black dog but is seen more commonly as a horse. There has, of course, been no opportunity to question a Pooka, but it seems likely that this faery would only account for a very small fraction of the total sightings of Black Dogs. This mischievous creature is notorious for tricksy behaviour that is often to the detriment of human witnesses, something that is not necessarily seen in the Black Dog.

As with the djinn, which also can take the form of a Black Dog and will appear later in the text, the Pooka is one of the creatures of faery that could be confused with a Black Dog but is not, in fact, a member of this class. Further reading in the text will make it clear that, while the Black Dog has some variation to its myths and stories, the apparition follows a set of behaviours and aspects of strangeness that help the researcher delineate it from other, similar creatures of folklore.

On another name note, one of the names that sometimes gets thrown out in discussion of Black Dogs is Cu Sith. W. Y. Evans-Wentz, in his classic book on the Fairy Faith, tells us about the Cu Sith, and we can quickly discern that this is not our subject either.

Cu Sith is Scots Gaelic for "faery dog", and Evans-Wentz notes that these hounds most often come in white with red ears, though they may sometimes be green. While it may be that the Phantom Black Dog might fall into the general class of the faery (more on this in the last section of the book), it is definitely not a Cu Sith.

In the folklore, Cu Sith seem to fall more into the Wild Hunt and/or trooping faery genre or theme than the Black Dog, which is solitary except in very rare instances.

Another thing to note about the Cu Sith is that, according to folklorist Theo Brown, the Cu Sith is most often sighted in Scotland, where the Black Dog is not as common. Given the territorial nature of the Black Dog, which emerges again and again throughout the text, this thought is not surprising.

TYPES

Theo Brown, in her extensive work "The Black Dog", has divided Black Dogs, which she considered to be apparitions, into three categories, aptly named A, B and C. The dictionary definition of an apparition is "the appearance of something remarkable or unexpected" and can include anything from the Black Dog to a sighting of the Blessed Virgin Mary.

Black Dog Type A may be called a "Barguest, Shuck, Black Shag, Trash, Skriker, Padfoot, Hooter and other names". Brown gives a list of the districts of England where she documented these sightings before going on to note that "all these creatures are ominous. Some are belligerent as well and many are associated with burial-sites and churchyards. The most striking characteristic of the Barguest type is that it goes out of its way to show the beholder it is no normal dog, but a monster from another world..."

In reading Brown's article, I was struck with the impression that Brown would very much like Type A Black Dog to go away since those apparitions interfered with her categorization of what she later calls "real" black dogs.

Nevertheless, she was compelled, as I am, to present this messy category since (a) the lore is very specific in naming them as Black Dogs, and (b) there is the possibility that some of the Dogs that refused to fit into Ms. Brown's neat definition of "true" Black Dogs may relate to other mysteries of a canine nature. Again, more on this thought will appear throughout the text, and we will discuss seemingly aggressive behaviour by these phantoms as we encounter it. Aggression is, after all, a matter of perspective.

Brown concludes that the Type A apparition can appear in a variety of forms but seems to prefer the Black Dog and that it is "malevolent in character". Honestly, from reading Brown's work several times through, it seems that Ms. Brown had a preconceived notion that a Black Dog was a beneficial road guardian and nothing more.

This view of the Black Dog as guardian was espoused by the earlier writer Ethel Rudkin, who wrote of her native Lincolnshire. The scarier apparitions of places like Norfolk do not fit Ms. Rudkin's assertions about the benevolent nature of the Black Dog. A review of all the different aspects of the Black Dog phenomenon throughout this book will leave the reader convinced that the Black Dog apparition cannot be easily assigned to any category of behaviour.

Brown is much more comfortable with the Type B and C Black Dogs, and given her original work on the lore of this phantom, it seems fair to use her definition of the Type B Dog as a beginning point for this adventure. It is worth documenting Ms. Brown's words extensively here:

> That which is nearly always known as the Black Dog, is always black and is always a dog and nothing else. It may appear like a normal dog ... It varies in size from normal – so that it is mistaken for a real dog – to enormous. The descriptions are remarkably consistent: "As big as a calf – donkey – Newfoundland – mastiff – two or three mastiffs" ... It is always associated with a definite place or "beat" on a road. It is always an individual ... Sometimes it is associated with a person or a family. If it is a family dog it haunts a house (or the vicinity), and seeing it usually means a member of the family living there will shortly die.

That is an awful lot of information to unpack, and it will be returned to in subsequent sections of the book.

Brown's final type of Dog, Type C, barely rates a mention since it is "rare" and "appears in a certain locality in conjunction with the calendar cycle". Brown mentions this type of Black Dog but does not provide examples, and I found no mention of this type of Black Dog, either as a legend or in a witness account, during my research.

Now, having looked at the "classic" definition of a Black Dog, let us look at some of the bits and pieces that can help us define our subject.

SIZE

As far as size, in the lore, almost all the Black Dogs appear as exactly what the name implies, a huge black dog. The notable exception to this feature is the Black Dog of the Hanging Hills, which will appear in a subsequent chapter. That particular dog was listed as the size of a spaniel. Brown speaks of the Newfoundland and mastiff, and one need only look up those breeds online to get an idea of how truly large a Black Dog might be.

For example, the Newfoundland, according to the AKC, can weigh as much as 130 to 150 pounds and stand a little over 28 inches at the shoulder. Mastiffs can be up to 30 inches at the shoulder and weigh a colossal 160 to 230 pounds. One really has to encounter one of these giant breeds to have a concept of just how massive they are.

I have personally lived with Irish wolfhounds, a very tall breed, and have known people with Great Danes, another very tall canine example. If any of these dogs – Newfoundland, mastiff, Irish wolfhound or Great Dane – were to run up to most people on a roadside, one suspects the person would be nervous until the dog expressed its intent. It is very difficult to be blasé about a dog that can come close to looking you in the eyes while standing on four paws.

Ethel Rudkin and Theo Brown both note that witnesses often report the Dog in question as being the size of a calf or even a donkey. Sometimes, the beast that their witnesses describe is said to be "table-high".

There are even accounts of the Black Dog changing sizes as the witness watches, such as the March 20, 2019, article on Lon Strickler's *Phantoms and Monsters* blog that details the story of a witness who saw a Dog expand to twice its starting size as it began to pursue the witness' car. Needless to say, the young lady in question departed the scene quickly, and the reader can learn more about the story in the chapter on the Black Dog as shape-shifter.

In summary, it seems safe to say that, in most instances, people who see the Black Dog see a canine large enough that the percipient's attention is grabbed and held immediately. Throughout the encounters reviewed in this text, you will see over and over again that the Dog in question was large enough to be beyond the norm and to really attract the witness' attention.

EYES

There certainly are Black Dogs that are reported with the normal dark eyes of a dog, but one of the effects that jumps out when you begin to investigate the sightings of these creatures is the prevalence, in multiple sources and stories, of glowing eyes.

By this, we do not simply mean eye shine but actual self-luminous eyes in either red, yellow or white, with the classic shade being red. Additionally, multiple sources over time often mention that the eyes of the Dog are "saucer-like" or "large as saucers". Additionally, the Black Dog is often described as staring, and this attention to the witness takes up a chapter of its own later in the book.

The subject of self-luminous eyes brings up another point of order. I will not attempt to make the Black Dog out to be an undiscovered species in this book. The creature is called a Phantom Black Dog for a reason, and the glowing eyes, along with other high strangeness aspects around these sightings, put the Black Dog firmly into the folkloric category of apparitions.

While the Black Dog is not a cryptozoological specimen, this does not mean that the Black Dog is harmless, as will be seen as the book progresses, nor that the Dog is incapable of interacting with its physical environment. How those physical interactions happen will be a matter of discussion in the Theories section of the book.

COLOUR

As we have noted, this apparition is black. Ethel Rudkin, the folklorist who really brought the Black Dog to the attention of the folklore community, had a witness, a "hard-headed" retired foreman who encountered the Dog several times and noted that no matter how dark the night was, one could always see the Dog because he was so much blacker.

This description of a beast that is darker than the night brings to mind the many reports of apparitions like shadow people and Alien Big Cats who are often described as "blacker than black". I will only deviate from the description of the Dog as black on a couple of occasions in the book, and those stories will be clear outliers.

COAT

Theo Brown states that the coat of the Black Dog may be described as "smooth and gleaming" but is more often "shaggy, like a bear". Rudkin reports that one Black Dog actually brushed against the witness, who testified that its coat was bristly, like the bristles of a pig.

SPEED

As one progresses through the tales, they will note that the Black Dog seems to be preternaturally swift. The phantom can often be seen trotting along beside a person walking, keeping pace with an individual on horseback or in a horse-drawn carriage, and even pacing a rider on a bicycle. It is not until the age of motor vehicles, though, that one truly begins to see that the Black Dog is no slowpoke.

A witness in Woodbridge, Suffolk, reporting on the website *Shuckland*, states that he sighted a Black Dog in early 1973 while riding a motorcycle:

> It was not bounding, leaping or running hard but seemed to glide smoothly and effortlessly in what I felt to be an unnatural manner ... as I was riding a motorcycle at about 30mph alongside this huge black dog, I was alarmed, and it ... "gave me the creeps", so I increased speed sharply to leave it behind. However, I found that it easily kept pace, still smoothly, and looked round at me as it did so, and, by this time ... thoroughly scared, I sped down the road, over the brow of the hill and down to Seckford Street. It was just over the brow of the hill that I lost sight of the dog [c.TM26404906.] Overall, the experience must have lasted over a distance of 400 to 600 yards, and I was so shaken by the meeting with the dog that I was white and shaking when I arrived home ... at ... St. John's Hill ...

So, this particular phantom kept pace with a rider on a motorbike who was exceeding thirty mph over a distance of 400 to 600 yards. The greyhound, which is extremely swift, is capable of speeds of forty-five mph over short distances, so the

Black Dog's speed might not be outside the realm of possibility until we take into account the size of the beast. No natural dog the size of a mastiff or Newfoundland should be capable of this kind of speed.

Additionally, in no story encountered in the research for this book did anyone ever outdistance a Black Dog, no matter what conveyance they were in. If you do run from the beast, it simply stays with you until it decides to disappear.

HABITAT

Theo Brown was a folklorist who compiled many Black Dog reports and gave readers an extensive rundown of this interesting phenomenon. According to this early writer on our topic, the most common feature of every Black Dog account was a road. The animals are most often spotted along roadsides or crossing roads and, in considering the stories, you will note that the Dog seems to appear and disappear from or through hedges, a distinctly English roadside embellishment, a great deal of the time.

Additionally, trees are mentioned often in Black Dog stories either as sites where the Dog appeared or disappeared or simply as landmarks to let the person hearing the story know where it took place. There are quite a number of stories that take one through forest land as well.

Brown, Rudkin, and later folklorist Ivan Bunn all mentioned the commonality of water in Black Dog stories. The Dog appears near ponds, streams, rivers, lakes and other bodies of water and can be found, in some stories, as the guardian of a bridge.

In the modern (1972) story of Graham Grant, an English coastguard who spotted a Black Dog that subsequently vanished before his eyes, the dog was on a beach at a place called Gorleston in Norfolk.

Brown goes on to note some accounts that are associated with churches and ecclesiastical buildings, such as church rectories, cemeteries, and graveyards, and with sites of violent death, including gallows. The very thorough folklorist even goes on to note that some families seem to be haunted by Black Dogs in much the same way that families in Ireland deal with the bean sidhe (or banshee), a fairy creature that appears periodically to predict a death in the family. There is an example of a family Black Dog in the death portent chapter of the book.

Finally, though the Black Dog seems to be a country apparition, for the most part, there are Dogs that seem to frequent certain cities and haunt the roads that lead out of them. We can see this particularly in the lore of the Latin American Black Dog, where a number of stories of the Cadejo, that region's Black Dog, take place in cities.

Brown also notes that there have been Black Dog reports near prehistoric remains such as standing stones and archeological sites. This is interesting in light of Linda Godfrey's fascinating work with the Manwolf and her conjectures about the association of these creatures with "Indian" mounds and other indigenous sacred sites in North America.

Having described the Black Dog's appearance and its habitat, some history of the Black Dog's progenitors seems to be in order.

2

A LITTLE CANINE HISTORY

THE ENGLISH FOLKLORIST W. P. Witcutt, writing in 1942, gives the opinion that Phantom Black Dog lore stems directly from pre-Christian "deities" such as Cerberus, the many-headed guardian of Hades in Greek mythology. I would question the status of Cerberus as a deity since there doesn't seem to be any evidence that said guard dog was worshipped, but I don't deny Witcutt's basic premise.

It seems clear that the Phantom Black Dog mythos is rooted in stories of dogs and dog-like beings told throughout history. In order to get closer to the roots of the Black Dog legend, one has to go back farther in time than even Ancient Greece.

Dogs have been human companions for about 11,000 years, according to Dr. Pontus Skøgland in an article on the BBC News website. While it might seem odd that humans chose a carnivore as a companion animal when you consider that humans were hunter-gathers in that time, the choice of canines makes more sense. If your very survival relies on bringing in game, what better companion than an animal with extraordinary senses that can help you find and, perhaps, bring down your prey.

Still, humans have had an ambivalent relationship with dogs

throughout the ages. Kiersten Carr, in "Hellhounds and Helpful Ghost Dogs", points out that, while dogs are commonly referred to as man's best friend and commended for their usefulness, loyalty and loving nature, there is still a deep strain of antipathy toward dogs that we see reflected in our language.

Carr gives examples of dogs not having much agency in folk tales, a place where the Black Dog tales certainly differ from other folklore, and bids us pay attention to our language and idioms around canines. Think of how insulting such epithets as dog, cur and bitch (or son of a bitch) are; how one works like a dog or is as sick as a dog; how an item is not fit for a dog or has gone to the dogs. A young, impudent person is often referred to derisively as a pup or puppy. If one is in trouble, one ends up in the doghouse and, when the final breath is drawn, depending on the circumstances, one may die like a dog.

While it is possible to see the supreme usefulness of the dog to a hunting and gathering society, sometimes actually serving as food in tough times, it also seems that the dog is not always viewed with the Pollyanna attitude that you might find on the websites or in the books of dog lovers. Indeed, the dog has been intimately linked with death since the beginnings of recorded history, and this connection certainly creates a direct link to our subject, as we shall see repeatedly throughout this text.

One might argue that the original Black Dog was an Egyptian god known to the peoples of the Nile as Anpu. In modern times, he is better known by his Greek name, Anubis, a name that will appear again later in this book. Anubis was "khentyamentiu, the foremost of the Westerners", i.e., the dead, who stood guard at the entrance to the Egyptian Underworld, Duat, and served as a psychopomp figure. In his role as a guide and guardian for the dead, he also served, with the Goddess Ma'at, in the judgement of those who have passed, helping with the decision to allow a soul into the afterlife or not.

Anubis is often depicted as a jackal-headed man (although archeologists now believe that he may have descended from a species of wolf indigenous to the area), but most interesting to us is his depiction as a smooth-coated black dog throughout Egyptian iconography. Even in these very early days, a Black Dog appears as a guardian between the worlds, and, though they are not as common as the shaggy-coated variety, the smooth coat does appear in some Black Dog sightings where the Dog is described as having a coat like a greyhound.

It should also be noted that the same variance in coat is noted by Manwolf researcher Linda Godfrey in her subject. The shaggy-coated Manwolves appear to be outdoor cryptids while the smooth-coated, Anubis variety of Manwolf likes to appear in the homes of witnesses. We do not see this site differentiation with Black Dogs of different coat types, however.

Another famous dog of history comes to us from the above-noted Greek myth of Hades and Cerberus. Adam Zmarzlinski, in his cultural analysis of Black Dog lore, points out that Cerberus is himself a creature of the in-between, born of the dragon Typhon, a monster of the heavens, and Echidna, a half-woman, half-snake known as the mother of all monsters and definitely a creature of the earth.

Cerberus was described as dusky in the literature and is depicted as black on Greek vases. He was said by Hesiod to have as many as fifty heads though most sources depict him with three heads, a serpent's tail and snakes growing from his spine. This fearsome creature's primary job was to serve as a one-way valve at the entrance to Hades, the Greek land of the dead. Souls were permitted to enter the realm, but they were not permitted to leave.

Again, we see this theme of the in-between, the liminal, in regard to this guardian who stands between the living and the dead and who is, himself, a creature of both earth and heaven.

We encounter yet another famous dog in Norse myths, Garm, the guardian of Hel. In Mark Norman's book *Black Dog Folklore*, the interesting fact is discovered that "in ancient Scandinavia, it was thought that dogs could follow the movements of the sinister death-goddess Hela. This makes the dog an intermediary factor between this world and the underworld."

Garm, the four-eyed guardian of Hel, the Norse land of the dead, not to be confused with the Christian place of torment, serves much the same function as did Anubis and Cerberus, standing watch at the gates of Hela's realm.

In the Eddic poem "Baldr's Dreams", one gets a wonderful poetic description of Garm, or some other hound of Hel, translated here by Alby Stone:

> *He met a hound that came from Hel.*
> *That one had blood upon his breast,*
> *and long did he bark at Baldr's father.*
> *Onward rode Odin – the earth-way roared –*
> *till he came to the high hall of Hel.*

I would presume, based on Garm's behaviour, that he was not happy with the All-Father coming into and then exiting the land of the dead. Even gods are supposed to obey the stricture that makes the entrance to Hel a one-way portal.

I will not belabour the point that all these famous dogs of myth are guardians of the in-between. In between death and life. In between this world and the Otherworld. In between what Patrick Harpur, author of *Daimonic Reality*, might call everyday reality and the imaginal realms. I will note that we will see this theme arise over and over through the text. Liminality clings to the Black Dog wherever that creature appears.

As a concluding note to this section, we can examine one other creature that might not be associated with the Black Dog until we begin to look, as Alby Stone did, at the original language of a legend.

In *Beowulf*, the villain is the uncanny creature Grendel. We are never quite clear what Grendel is, but when the root language is examined, one finds that he is called a "scucca", which is usually translated "demon". Interestingly, "scucca" is also thought to be the derivation for one of the most famous Black Dog names, Black Shuck.

Even more interestingly, the story tells us that Grendel's eyes shone with a "fire-like, baleful light", a description that will be seen over and over again in the Black Dog lore. Finally, Grendel and his mother are both referred to as "brimwylf" or water wolf in the text. In the section on location, it will be noted that Black Dogs are frequently sighted near bodies of water, and, indeed, they sometimes appear from said bodies. There is even a legend of a Black Dog appearing from the mouth of a large fish caught from a pond.

Could Grendel have been a Black Dog? Readers of this classic will probably object that Grendel is spoken of as having arms and that he spent a lot of time talking to himself, something Black Dogs are not known to do.

Still, the presence of this creature who guards a burial mound in marshland certainly meshes with the historical context of the Phantom Black Dog. A marsh is neither solid land nor completely water, and a burial mound is, of course, an entrance into the land of the dead, neither here nor there.

You note throughout all of the accounts above that the dog moves from god to guardian of the underworld. Perhaps, Grendel and the Black Dog of lore were the next steps in this demotion process, in which the loyal guardian now becomes a reviled killer or, at least, a portent of death.

3
_____

HELLHOUND?

As the research for this book progressed, I noted that, as I reviewed newer sources, the use of the names hellhound, demon dog or devil dog (I'll use hellhound here to refer to all these titles) seemed to become more popular. After thoroughly researching this phenomenon, I do not believe that those monikers are suitable, and I will not use them in this text.

My reasoning is based on my belief that the classic Black Dog that we will be studying is not a demonic phenomenon, a position that I will support in the Theories section of the book. I further base my reticence on using these titles on four disparate elements that seem to me to have contributed to the use of the name. I will deal with these four elements briefly before we plunge into the lore.

The first and most modern of the reasons for the use of hellhound is something with which all my readers will be intimately familiar – media sensationalism.

Mark Norman, in his terrific book *Black Dog Folklore*, notes that the scarier forms of the Black Dog legend are often the ones that get the most attention, particularly in the media. It is sometimes said of TV newscasts that "If it bleeds, it leads", and it seems that something similar can be said of print and web journalists looking to hook readers.

Why focus on the harmless or, in fact, beneficial forms of the Black Dog legend, which will be examined, when you can get the reader's attention with articles about scary hellhounds?

A massive canine skeleton was recovered in an archeological dig near Leiston Abbey in Suffolk, and Norman uses this instance as a mini case study of the sensationalization of the modern press.

Norman notes that the coverage, which began with a simple item of interest in an archeological journal, developed into a worldwide sensation when some enterprising reporter linked the local Black Dog lore with the skeleton.

Other journalistic outlets played up terrifying stories like the Black Dog of Bungay, which will be covered later, and began to refer to the giant dog as a hellhound even though there was nothing to indicate that there was anything supernatural about the found skeleton. Notably absent from the press coverage was any notion that the Black Dog might be an object of anything but terror and that the plain fact of the matter was that the dog in question was simply a large mastiff-like canine that likely guarded the monastery.

In the same way, many paranormal TV shows also have a strong tendency to "hype" their subject matter by making everything from ghosts to UFOs and lake monsters scary. Of course, it must be realized that these shows are supposed to be entertainment and not documentary fact, but they do influence the way that the public sees various phenomenon and, more and more, those views are tainted by fear.

In other words, a hellhound is interesting and scary and, therefore, entertaining, and a Phantom Black Dog is just another boring creature from folklore. While our subject has been blamed for causing harm to humans and has even been implicated in their deaths, as shall be seen, these stories are not common, and many of those that do exist are questionable.

The use of the term hellhound as a sensational lead for the media moves right into my next point about the use of the term to describe the Phantom Black Dog. Human nature dictates that we demonize that which scares us.

Though Black Dogs seldom interact physically with people, witnesses often report the sort of abject terror experienced by many percipients of the paranormal. This fear is increased when the Dog behaves aggressively by growling, barking and snarling. This sort of behaviour seems to be seen most often in stories where the Dog is intent on keeping a person from going a particular way for reasons that only the Black Dog knows. If it scares people, then, in many human minds, it must be evil, and an evil phantom becomes a demon very quickly in some people's thoughts.

As I've noted, we will explore the demonic explanation for Black Dogs in detail later in the book, but, for now, let's note this idea and move on.

The third reason for the hellhound moniker relates to the second, fear and demonization. One of the cycles of life that humans fear the most is death, and Black Dogs are associated, even in the minds of those not intimately familiar with them, with death, dying and the dead.

Barbara Woods, in her article "The Devil in Dog Form", recounts some stories about the "window pane dog" of the Canton of Uri in Switzerland. This creature is a huge, shaggy black dog with enormous, glowing eyes (thus its odd name) that appears on roadsides and walks with travelers. I'm not certain why the people of the canton were so frightened by this beast, but Woods goes on to elucidate.

Apparently, the window pane dog is associated with "restless soul of an untruthful councilman, or of a shyster, or of a blasphemer ..." Woods goes on to say, on this subject:

> Many commentators see a survival of the ancient idea of the transmigration of souls in one of the common modern beliefs about the dog: namely, that he embodies a restless soul. Restless souls are the ghosts of wicked people such as cruel noblemen, murderers, suicides, traitors, witches – and all manner of godless people who might be considered the devil's accomplices. Also included amongst the restless souls are those who have met a violent death, and have gone to their end "unhousel'd, unanointed, unanel'd" and hence also have joined the devil's throng. These ghosts very frequently take on the form of a dog.

Given that Black Dogs are sometimes associated with gibbets and other death sites and that they almost certainly can be said to be death portents, at times, one cannot completely ignore this line of thought.

Certainly, the Black Dog that was, according to legend, said to haunt Newgate Prison, just inside the city of London, and that was said to walk after every execution at the prison is an example of a Black Dog legend linked to violent death. The story arose after a "sorcerer" allegedly died under horrible circumstances while awaiting trial at the prison. While the tale appears to be fictional, it brings forth the continuing association of our subject with the dead and, particularly, the restless dead.

I certainly can't deny the association of the Black Dog with the passing of humans. In fact, I devote a whole chapter of this book to the Black Dog as a portent of death and go on to discuss cases where the Dog is said to have caused injury or death. However, this link to the dead is only a part of this intricate lore, and I feel it must be taken in the complete context of that lore.

The relationship between the Black Dog and death does not require us to name the Dog a hellhound, but there is one final piece of this puzzle that explains a lot about why a dog and, particularly, a black dog might be an object of horror to some people.

In the trials of those people accused of magical practices in the Middle Ages and right up to the Witch Trials at Salem, we see one figure creep into the "testimony" of the alleged witches repeatedly: the familiar.

A familiar was a helping spirit, often seen in the form of an animal, that assisted sorcerers, witches, and cunning folk in their magical work. The typical witch "confession" usually involved a pact with the Devil, often sealed with an obscene kiss. The Devil would then often give the witch a familiar. Conversely, the familiar might appear to the witch and lead them off to their first meeting with the Devil at a sabbat, a meeting of witches.

Familiars could take human form, but often they took the form of an animal that one might find commonly in a home, anything from a cat to a rat to a goat to a dog. The creature was often supposed to be black, so we can see why the medieval imagination might immediately push all black dogs into the realm of familiars. As the familiar was intimately associated with its supposed true master, the Devil, it is easy to see why to this day, black dogs, like black cats, have a harder time getting adopted from animal rescues than other coloured pets.

This association of the black dog, or our subject Black Dog, with the Devil runs into several issues. The foremost of these issues is that history shows us that the confessions elicited from "witches" were obtained through torture and that those tortured often had nothing at all to do with witches or the Devil. In fact, they were more likely to be people who owned a spot of land that someone else wanted or a village eccentric who had become a scapegoat for a run of bad luck in the local settlement. The lurid tales told of witches had far more to do with the over-heated imaginations of the inquisitors than they did with fact.

We will talk more about actual magical practitioners later in the book, but, for now, I feel that we can safely say that the hell-hound moniker is not a title that the Phantom Black Dog wears deservedly.

SECTION TWO
LOCATION, LOCATION, LOCATION

Types of places associated with appearances of
black dogs include: roads, crossroads, lanes,
footpaths, bridges, gateways, doorways,
staircases, boundaries, fields, hedges, green
lanes, prehistoric and treasure sites, wayside
burials, churchyards, graves and gallows,
wells, trees, and places where tragic events
have occurred ...

Simon Sherwood
Black Dogs of England

4

HIGHWAYS AND BYWAYS

WHILE IT IS NOT POSSIBLE, given space considerations, to cover every location where a Phantom Black Dog has been seen, this section of the book will endeavour to show some of the more common habitats of the Black Dog and provide some accounts illustrating those common sites.

To begin, every author on this subject has commented, at one point or the other, that the most common place to meet a Black Dog is on a road or lane. In the typical witness scenario, the person is walking, riding or driving along such a road or lane or sometimes a footpath. The Black Dog either simply appears or seems to come through a hedge, often with a sound like "twigs crackle as if they were afire". The Dog will then pace the witness and either vanish, make its way back through the hedge, or even disappear into a tree or into the ground.

In those cases where the Dog appears to be a normal creature, this notion is often disabused when the witness either sees the Dog vanish, or tries to peek through the hedge and cannot find the Dog anywhere. Several of the accounts end with a person going into their home and telling someone about the interesting dog that followed them home, only to be unable to find the animal when the witness comes back out of doors.

As an example of this sort of story, we can begin with an upstanding witness, a Methodist lay preacher. A quick note on these itinerant preachers is in order. In the early days of the Methodist church, John Wesley, its founder, credentialed laypeople to preach and lead worship due to the simple fact that there were more people who wanted to worship than there were ordained ministers to serve them. This resulted in lay preachers who worked a circuit, going from place to place, leading worship as they went.

Ethel Rudkin tells us that Mr. C, the preacher's son, testified that his father was a man of "exceptional physique and an iron nerve". This manly preacher was returning home of a winter's evening from his duties on the Alford Circuit and had to go down a road called Mumby Long Lane, between the villages of Hogsthorpe and Willoughby, Lincolnshire. The preacher had a "most unusual and uncanny feeling" and nearly decided not to go that way before determining that there was no other path to home.

As the lay preacher walked, a Black Dog appeared at his side and paced the whole length of that long lane with him. The preacher tried to run the animal off, but it would not be moved. It disappeared at the end of the lane, and the preacher, naturally, asserted that the Dog was sent that night to protect him from "something or someone who had no good intentions toward him".

While this might be an example of a guardian Black Dog, there is never any indication that the threat in the story was anywhere other than the preacher's mind. The account is, however, an excellent example of a road-walking Dog that appears and disappears in very specific locations.

More typical is this tale, from the *Shuckland* website, related by an eighty-two-year-old gentleman who was told the story by his father:

> I am 82 years of age, and my father told me this story. He lived in Overstrand and was courting my mother, who lived in Cromer. He had been to see her one night and was on his way home [along the B1159], about 12 o'clock. When he looked down at his side, there walking beside him was a large black shaggy dog. Not wanting it to follow him home he struck at it with his walking stick, which to his amazement passed clean through the animal's body. He told me, "I took to my heels and ran like hell." My father was not a drinking man or given to telling tall stories.

In this tale, the Dog appears and simply walks beside the percipient. Given what we have seen of Black Dog behaviour, if the witness had not tried to hit the dog with a stick and scared himself silly, one imagines the Dog would have accompanied him for a distance and then vanished. We will see that Black Dogs seem to always be able to shrug off blows as we proceed with this work.

It is not just pedestrians who see Black Dogs. In this sighting, also from the *Shuckland* website, a cyclist spies the elusive beast:

> I was cycling along Poppylot Road between Feltwell and Southery at about midnight on a fine moonlight night [in the 1930s] when two green eyes came into the beam of my front light followed by a large black dog running towards me in the centre of the road and dragging a heavy rattling chain. The dog stayed on course in the centre of the road and showed no interest as I cycled past. Apart from the unusually large size of both dog and chain it did not differ from any other dog ... If it

was Old Shuck that [I] ... encountered he just went on his way
and ignored [me] ...

This witness was prepared to believe that this was a sighting
of an ordinary dog except that the dog was remarkably large and
dragging a heavy chain, a feature seen in the Shuck-type sightings common to the district of Norfolk. The author of the
website also notes that there were two other Black Dog sightings
in the same area. As Black Dogs seem to be quite territorial, the
additional sightings gave some credence to this cyclist's
encounter.

It is intriguing that the witness saw the dog head-on, coming
toward him, and that the Dog was not at all concerned with his
presence. As will be seen in a later chapter, a Black Dog ignoring
a witness is somewhat unusual. Perhaps this Dog was on its way
to keep an appointment with some other road walker?

One of the things of note as we peruse more and more of
these stories is that, while the Black Dog often paces along the
side of a road, it is also known to cross the road, just like any
number of Sasquatch that have been caught out by motorists. In
later chapters of the book, the reader will even encounter
seeming collisions and near collisions with Black Dogs. In the
following case, however, the Black Dog seems intent on
completely impeding progress down the road.

In an account from Madeleine Dahlgren's *South Mountain
Magic*, she relates the story of William L., who lived in a hut "not
over a quarter mile from the alleged habitat of the Black Dog".
The Black Dog of this Maryland (US) locale has the wonderfully
evocative name of Snarly Yow.

William L was returning to his home one night, around 10:00
p.m., after going to the village "to make some small purchases
for his family". The witness reported that the night was clear
and starlit as he came upon a huge Black Dog blocking the road.

Snarly Yow was larger than any dog he had ever seen and blocked the road, preventing his homeward progress.

William wasn't having any of that and got down from the wagon to remove the Dog from his path by force. Imagine the poor man's confusion when, as he attempted to strike Snarly Yow, the apparition grew in size. William's attempts to beat the animal into submission were basically an exercise in shadow-boxing, as the man could make no contact with the impediment before him.

After a time, the Black Dog moved on, and William went on his way, tuckered out from swinging at nothing but otherwise unharmed. This apparition's habit of blocking roads and lanes and even entries to certain areas makes me wonder what causes this behaviour.

In at least one instance we will see further on in the book, a Black Dog blocking forward progress may have saved a man's life. Could the Black Dog be acting in its guardian function when it keeps people from proceeding? Or is it simply being territorial? I propose that the behaviour may be either, depending on the situation.

Another road-blocking Black Dog appeared to a witness in England in 1905, and his account appears in the *Journal of Psychical Research* in 1908:

In the beginning of January, 1905, about half-past seven in the evening, I was walking up from the Halfway [a local inn]. I suddenly saw an animal that seemed to be like a large, black dog appear quite suddenly out of the hedge and run across the road quite close in front of me; I thought it was the dog belonging to the curate. I was just going to call it to send it home, when it suddenly changed its shape, and turned into a black donkey standing on its hind legs. This creature had two glowing eyes, which appeared to me to be almost as big as saucers. I looked at it in astonishment for a minute or so, when it suddenly vanished. After that I hurried home, for the sight of this creature with the large shining eyes gave me a shock. The evening was a light one for the time of year.

This business of changing into a donkey standing on its hind legs is something that we will encounter in subsequent chapters. Theo Brown's Barguest type of Black Dog is known to assume more shapes than just the Black Dog form, and the donkey is one of them. Standing on hind legs is also something that is not unknown in Black Dog lore, but upright posture is rare in the traditional stories.

While this chapter contains just a sampling of Black Dog road encounters, it will become clear to the reader how common the highways and byways are to this phantom as the text progresses. The Black Dog will be encountered on so many variations of roads that one will have little doubt that the creature loves the paths of human travel and frequents them.

For now, however, it is time to investigate another common association for the Black Dog: its frequent proximity to water.

5

WATER, WATER, EVERYWHERE

ANOTHER QUITE COMMON note in the lore of the Black Dog and one that is mentioned by many commentators is the phantom's seeming love for the water.

Folklorist Ivan Bunn, in an analysis of some of his cases in a delightful newsletter called the *Lantern* (from the age when one typed the newsletter, mimeographed copies and sent it out by snail mail for a small fee), noted that almost every story he had collected happened within five miles of water. He goes on to provide a table showing that the stories increase in frequency as one draws closer to a water source.

Ivan Bunn also gives the following water-related story that came to him in personal correspondence and which he shared with the *Shuckland* website. Occurring in December 1972, this account finds the witness fishing "on the beach near the foot of the West Runton slipway", another site in the Norfolk district of the UK, in the early morning hours.

The witness became aware of movement near a cliff on the Cromer side of the slipway. The moving object was an enormous Black Dog that the percipient compared to the size of a Great Dane, another very large breed of dog that averages thirty to thirty-two inches at the shoulder for males. It had a "head that was huge and very broad relative to the body, and as it got closer, he saw a very short muzzle, and ears that were quite small and bent-over".

The witness thought the Dog might be from the village and, at first, tried to call it to him. The Black Dog ignored him completely, seemingly totally taken up with the search for something as it moved back and forth along the foot of the cliff. The witness reported that the creature got to within fifteen feet of him and "it made no sound even on shingle, and cast no shadow".

The witness observed the Dog for at least fifteen minutes then "got cold, went home, and told his wife about the encounter".

One could be forgiven for thinking this actually was a dog from the village, but a couple of items belie this point. First, the witness notes that the creature was soundless, "even on shingle". If you've ever walked a beach with slate shingles or the like, you will know that ambulating quietly is nearly impossible.

The fisherman also notes that the Black Dog cast no shadow, a detail that gives one pause. We're told that the event happened early in the day but not whether the day was cloudy. I would think though that a large, seemingly solid dog should have cast some sort of shadow, even on a grey day.

The witness also seems to have had an atypical reaction to this mystery animal. There is none of the frequent terror reaction that is often found in Black Dog sightings but, instead, a sort of blasé attitude where the witness seems to shrug and walk away. Even more odd, the witness then seems to find the event important enough to report to his wife, once he is away from the Black Dog entirely.

One sees this same "looking for something" behaviour in our next water-related account.

In the famous 1972 sighting of Coastguard Graham Grant, a sighting that was detailed in the *Eastern Daily Press* as well as appearing on the British television show *Animal X*, the witness was on duty at the Gorleston rescue headquarters in Norfolk, UK. Mr. Grant testifies that:

> Looking to the north at about 4.45am, at daybreak, on Wednesday last, April 19th, I saw a large, black hound-type dog on the beach, about a quarter of a mile north of the lookout. What made me look was that the dog was running, then stopping, as if looking for someone. I watched it for one to two minutes and then it vanished before my eyes. I kept on looking for a time but it did not reappear.

The witness also noted that the beach had recently been flattened by bulldozers, so there was nowhere for the dog to hide. The coastguard had just moved to Norfolk, so he was not familiar with the stories of Black Shuck until he mentioned the sighting to some of his peers.

In an interesting side note, the Black Dog known as Shuck is said, in Norfolk folklore, to be a harbinger of doom and of storms. Shortly after the encounter, a strong northwest gale hit that section of the coastline, so we have a storm and an event that would certainly be viewed as a potential disaster by search and rescue personnel.

Ethel Rudkin tells us that, in her native Lincolnshire, there was a Black Dog that frequented an area called Old Yard Close. The area was bounded by an old road on the west and a new road to the north. As with many of our road-haunting Black Dogs, this one refused to walk the new road but, instead, frequented the old road, which went past the "top of the Fishpond".

That pond was spring fed from a hillside to the east of the

road. The spring flowed under the road to the pond. This is also a case of a Dog that disappeared into a tree, in this case, an ash that "stood at the end of the next lane running west, a little farther along toward Grayingham".

The *Shuckland* website, a cornucopia of Black Dog sightings both historical and modern, speaks of the following sighting in 1967:

> Mr. Jack Disney, then aged about 52, was walking from West Horndon to Brentwood [Essex] in August 1967, on a footpath through Thorndon Park. As he approached a pool known as the "Horse Pond", at nearly midnight, he saw a large brown dog coming towards him, and going south. He described it as about the size of a Great Dane, with "eyes of fire", and felt it to be "threatening". It passed him by as he drew level with the pond [TQ61569073.]

This Dog is listed as brown but given the size of the beast and the eyes of fire, one might be willing to say that our subject had an off-colour day. This creature with "eyes of fire" was also a harbinger of death, as the witness' elder brother died of a heart attack a week or so later, and a year later his wife, who was only in her forties, died of a hemorrhagic stroke. The association of the Phantom Black Dog with death is a famous one and one to which we will return in a subsequent chapter. The scientific materialist will cry coincidence, but, later on, we will look at the numbers.

The author, Christopher Marlowe, shares his Black Dog encounter in his book *People and Places in Marshland*. The writer was lodging in a cottage beyond the marches in Stiffkey, Norfolk. He had heard of the Black Dog legends rife in the area and decided that he would spend the night out in a nearby marsh, determined to get a glimpse of the creature.

The night was lit by a half moon, and he placed himself in a "hollow beside a pool not far from the high tide mark". His hopes were answered. An "indefinable shadow" showed up on the horizon and was followed by "the most appalling howl". The shadow resolved itself into a classic Black Dog, huge, black and red-eyed, which, as with some of our stories above, seemed to be searching for something.

Marlowe was fairly certain he was the prey du jour and fled for his cottage, certain he was being pursued. He had to get someone to open the door for him, and as he tried to raise the attention of those in the house, he testifies that he felt the creature's "scorching breath" on him and saw its "ferocious eyes".

Marlowe was saved by someone opening the door. He fell through in the nick of time, the Dog's "great black body" seemed to leap at him but, instead, slammed heavily into the door, a good example of the Black Dog sometimes having an effect on its physical surroundings.

It almost seems that this Black Dog was determined to teach Mr. Marlowe a lesson about the old adage "Be careful what you ask for". I find it peculiar that Marlowe could feel the hounds "scorching breath" and even see its eyes but, as we see so often in these stories, the Black Dog let him be until he had made his escape. I am minded of Linda Godfrey's Manwolf stories, where the creature gives chase but never actually runs down the witness though it seems quite capable of doing so.

D. A. McManus, in his book *The Middle Kingdom*, tells the 1928 story of his close personal friend. This is one of a few Black Dog stories out of Ireland and happened in County Londonderry in Northern Ireland. The witness was a student at Trinity College, Dublin, but, on this day, was doing a bit of fishing from a creek.

The young man's angling was disturbed by the sound of an animal approaching, splashing along heavily in the creek, and, when he caught sight of the creature, he sought immediate refuge up a tree, a clear display of the abject terror that we see in many Black Dog cases. The student describes an enormous black beast with "fierce red eyes" that carried with it an intense sense of menace.

The witness stayed up the tree for some time, afraid that the animal might double back and attack him. When he finally screwed up his courage to come down from the tree, he packed his gear and vacated the fishing hole. When he came back later with armed relatives, there was no sign of the fierce animal.

This tale shows the Black Dog interacting with its physical environment, in this case making splashing sounds in the creek, and we also see here the classic "fierce red eyes".

In Katharine Briggs' encyclopedic work on British folk tales, there is the story of Adam, which will be covered in the chapter on the Black Dog's association with death. Adam met his Black Dog while crossing bridges, presumably over water obstacles along the road, and this Dog was anything but harmless.

Finally, we can come to America for another "hellhound" (please see the chapter titled Hellhound? for my thoughts on that moniker) that has a definite association with water and has been covered by Linda Godfrey and Chad Lewis as well as highlighted on the TV show *Monsters and Mysteries in America*, season 3, episode 6. I'll use the witness narrative from the television show for the basis of this section.

Monsters and Mysteries had two sets of witnesses to the phenomenon at the Meridean Island, Wisconsin (US), boat landing. Both sets of witnesses described a dense, cold fog rolling in and the sudden feeling that something was amiss. One of the witnesses even claimed that he felt anxious before he ever arrived at the boat landing.

In both events, the witnesses first heard growls coming from the fog and very quickly decided to leave the area. Two of the witnesses reported seeing the apparition of a woman who was supposedly drowned in this region and a ragged-looking Black Dog with glowing red eyes. Both sets of witnesses fled for their lives and only escaped the phenomenon when they were well clear of the boat landing and moving onto the main road.

Again, we see a Black Dog breaking off its pursuit at a seemingly specific spot. This apparent territory and refusal to travel beyond the territory is a trait that we will see throughout these pages. Theo Brown, in her seminal work on Black Dog folklore, emphasizes this idiosyncrasy of the Black Dog as one of her defining characteristics of the apparition.

I am intrigued by a couple of interesting features of this witness testimony.

First, I noted that both sets of witnesses recalled a dense, cold fog rolling in before the events occurred. This matter of strange mists appearing in relation to paranormal phenomena is explored in depth in Linda Godfrey's *Monsters Among Us*, but suffice to say that these fogs have been noted by other researchers.

Secondly, for those who love to play with names and their significance, there is also the strange name resemblance between Meridean, Wisconsin, and Meriden, Connecticut, where another Black Dog is found. I am not quite sure what to make of this resemblance, but my intuition tells me that this is a subject that bears further investigation.

While there certainly seem to be a number of stories that relate our subject to water, Janet and Colin Bord in their *Alien Animals* seem unconvinced. While several authors on the Black Dog legend conclude that water has a role to play in the sightings, the Bords note that, in the British Isles, at least, it is the rare place where one is not near water unless there is a drought.

I personally fall into the middle ground on this topic. In looking through the scanter lore of Black Dogs in the US and

Canada, water does not appear to play as important a role in the documented sightings, but then we come across stories like the one on Meridean Island, which happens at a boat landing on a river.

Given the careful analysis that some writers have done on this topic, it seems best not to gainsay them and to at least accept the possibility of the Black Dog's connection to water. I will explore some esoteric theories of our subject in later chapters, but the subject of water also brings up a footnote about still ponds, lakes and pools that I wanted to emphasize.

Many people interested in Forteana, and especially in lake monsters, are familiar with the story of Boleskine House, a dwelling near the legendary Loch Ness, where the equally legendary occultist Aleister Crowley lived and performed an operation called the Sacred Magic of Abramelin. This magical working is designed to invoke one's Holy Guardian Angel, in ceremonial magic, the spiritual guide to all one's later working.

It is alleged that the modern era of Loch Ness monster sightings started around the time that Crowley resided at the house and was actively working. The interesting thing to note here is that John Michael Greer, a Golden Dawn ceremonial magician and author of a book on monster lore, maintains that the presence of still, cold water, an apt description of Loch Ness, encourages what he calls etheric manifestations.

We will run across manifestations in the Theories section of the book, but suffice to say here that an etheric manifestation would be an example of a being of the Otherworld moving to our world and assuming some form. The Loch Ness monster could simply be an Otherworld entity that decided to take advantage of the opportune circumstances – still, cold water and a thinning of the Veil Between the Worlds – to manifest.

For our purposes, we have noted that the Phantom Black Dog is known to appear near ponds and other still bodies of water, so a similar mechanism for the apparition's appearance could be working in some of our cases.

While this interesting theory gives further weight to the link between Black Dogs and water, the presence of a body of water is not the near universal aspect of a sighting that a road or path is. Additionally, we have sightings of the Black Dog near the ocean – certainly not a cold, still body of water. Let's place the presence of water in these stories into the hypothesis pile and move on.

When one begins to examine Black Dog sightings in cemeteries, churchyards, and other places of burial, one finds themselves on much firmer ground.

6

DEFENDER OF THE DEAD

KATHARINE BRIGGS and Ruth Tongue both note that there is a folkloric tradition of Black Dogs protecting cemeteries and churchyards in Britain and the Scandinavian countries. As there appeared to be a belief that the first person buried in a church-yard was obliged to watch over the place, a subsequent tradition arose that a black dog be buried in the northern part of a churchyard to watch over the cemetery. In this way, a human's soul would not have the guardian duty, and thus we have the origins of the legend of the Church Grim.

Archeologists are conflicted about whether there is actually any evidence for belief in the Grim, but the stories are firmly anchored in the folklore, often with a theme of keeping the minister out of the way while the caretaker of the churchyard did what had to be done. As a dog lover, I find this business of sacrificing a dog to avoid human guardianship of a graveyard distasteful, but I see why it developed if that was truly the operant belief system. Mark Norman relates at least one such story in his book on the Black Dog.

Whether the Church Grim legend is true, there is ample

evidence placing the Black Dog at the scene of churchyards, cemeteries and other places of burial.

The story of the Demon Dog of Valle Crucis is related in the introduction to this work. While that particular story is most likely an urban legend, it may have some basis in fact. Writer on the paranormal, Brent Swancer, tells of two other stories that he located about this particular "Demon Dog", one on Reddit and the other a witness report he received after writing an article on Black Dogs. That witness' testimony is worth hearing.

According to Swancer, the witness stated that she and her husband were driving past the Valle Crucis church, St. John's Episcopal, "an ancient looking stone church that sits alongside Highway 194 and butts up against a spooky graveyard overgrown with trees and weeds that choke the old, crumbling grave-stones". The couple were proceeding past the church and its graveyard one evening when something dark appeared in the middle of the road, requiring them to hit the brakes. The observer, who wanted to remain anonymous, said:

> It was a very large, black form, as big as a bear, hunched over, heaving as if it were taking very big breaths. We actually thought it was a bear at first, but then it looked up and we could see that it had a sort of reddish glow to its eyes and a distinctive canine look. It looked sort of like a mastiff, but much larger, all muscular and bunched up, with scraggly hair stuck up in all directions. Then, without warning it came running at us at full speed. There was no time for us to get the car into gear and escape, this thing was bearing down on us. And just as we braced for impact, it just wasn't there anymore. It had vanished. And that was that.

The article was published in 2019, so we must assume that the sighting was relatively recent. In the course of this text, you will see several instances of Black Dog near misses with cars and even instances where the motorist thought they struck the Dog. In none of these accounts was any physical evidence found, either in the form of Black Dog traces or damage to the vehicle.

As with the urban legend of this Black Dog, the creature appears as the couple pass the church and its graveyard, but, instead of pursuing the witnesses out of its territory, the Dog seems to bluff charge these people and then disappears. It should be noted that the result is the same; in both the urban legend and this witness statement, the Dog scares the witnesses away from its demesne, and one wonders if these good people changed their routes after this incident.

The Black Dog that seems to haunt the church in Valle Crucis is not the only American example of this phenomenon. Thomas White, in his *Ghosts of Southwestern Pennsylvania*, cites a church and a Quaker meeting house in his area of interest that have Black Dog legends attached to them.

While White does not record any witness testimony, he does note that people approaching the gates of the church and attached cemetery experience menacing growls and that some have reported sighting a Black Dog that was bold enough to approach their car. The same observations were reported for the nearby Quaker meeting house.

Also in the United States, Linda Godfrey, in her *Monsters of Wisconsin* book, speaks of Phantom Black Dogs that haunt Okauchee Lake in Waukesha County. These creatures are the usual oversized, red-eyed variety that we have seen so often in this text, but Godfrey states that one of the notable things about the lake is that it used to house an "ancient, thirty-foot conical burial mound as well as other sites sacred to Native Americans". While these mounds certainly are not churchyards or cemeteries, they do qualify as burial sites as well as being tied into the religion of those who created them.

I doubt that it is any coincidence that so much high strangeness happens in lands that have an aboriginal connection. The traditional spirituality of First Nations people is shamanic and animistic. The traditional people of these tribes have a deep connection to the spirits of their land, and this is a subject that will be investigated in the final part of the book.

Moving "across the pond" to the British Isles, there are a surfeit of burial place stories to choose from. Ethel Rudkin starts off our perusal of these accounts with a simple tale of a Black Dog that manifests close to a church:

> At Algarkirk, Mrs. B., who lives there, has seen the Black Dog near the three trees that grow close to the church. It is tall and thin, with a long neck and pointed nose. It leaps into the road and runs before the spectator, leaping over another gate farther on. It always comes and goes on one's left. "I once heard the leaves rustle as it jumped through," said Mrs. B. (Per Mr. Nussey, Boston)

The referenced church is likely the parish Church of St. Peter and St. Paul. Interestingly, this Black Dog seems to have borne a resemblance to something closer to a greyhound and not the usual, massive, red-eyed canine related in the lore. It's also intriguing to note the leaf-rustling noise the beast made, presumably as it jumped through a hedge, a possible sign of physical interaction with the environment.

Though not a churchyard, another story from Rudkin relates to the legend of Black Dogs haunting execution sites. This Black Dog haunted a gallows site near the Parish of Tring.

The legend of the site was that in 1751, an old woman suspected of witchcraft was drowned. In that time, it was believed that the body of a witch would be rejected by water, one of God's creations, and that, therefore, the witch would float higher in the water than a "normal" person. Safety precautions were taken to ensure that the accused could be retrieved, but it seems that, in this instance, the accused witch was accidentally drowned.

The chimney sweep responsible for this atrocity, presumably because he made the accusation, was later hanged and gibbeted. Gibbeting is the practice of hanging the corpse of a convict in chains as an object lesson to the community. A Black Dog was seen at the gibbet site long after the body was finally taken down and presumably buried nearby.

Rudkin brings the account up to a more modern date by giving the tale of a village schoolmaster who saw the Dog. The teacher was returning home in a gig, a light, two-wheeled carriage, with another person driving and, when the two came near the spot where the gibbet had once stood, they saw a "flame of fire as large as a man's hat" on the roadside. The gig driver pulled the horses to a stop and hushed the schoolmaster as the teacher started to ask questions.

The schoolmaster then goes on to relate:

I then saw an immense black dog lying on the road, just in front of our horse, which also appeared trembling with fright. The dog was the strangest looking creature I ever beheld. He was as big as a Newfoundland, but very gaunt, shaggy, with long ears and tail, eyes like balls of fire, and large, long teeth, for he opened his mouth and seemed to grin at us. He looked more like a fiend than a dog, and I trembled as much as my companion. In a few minutes the dog disappeared, seeming to vanish like a shadow, or sink into the earth, and we drove on over the spot where he had lain.

This sighting is fascinating. The Black Dog does not manifest right away but first appears as a flame on the side of the road. The appearance of lights and "fairy fire" is not a phenomenon tied to the Black Dog in the lore despite the appearance of anomalous lights in the presence of other high strangeness (see Cutchin and Renner's extensive discussion of lights in reference to Sasquatch, in their *Where the Footprints End* series).

I would also note that this Dog appeared to grin at the witnesses. This attention to the percipient is something we will see repeatedly, as is the placement of a Black Dog such that it blocks the road and prevents travel. Travel by gig seems to have been a somewhat hazardous mode of travel, so I have to wonder, again, if our Black Dog was not assuming our guardian role. Perhaps this carriage was travelling faster than was safe?

Christopher Reeve, in his book *A Straunge and Terrible Wunder*, brings us the testimony of Mrs. A. M. Wilson, who is relating an incident that happened to her father:

Recounting an incident closer to Bungay, Mrs. A. M. Wilson of Beccles, writes: "This incident happened some 60 years ago to my late father, and I heard the story from him more than once ... The incident took place at Earsham ...one night shortly before Xmas, and very near to midnight ... Father had arrived in Bungay [from Norwich] shortly before 12pm after finishing work in a Norwich bakery late. This left him to walk the last mile to the village ... there was thick snow on the ground, and a bright clear moonlit sky.

"As he approached the last of the first row of cottages known as Temple Bar [at c.TM326893], he said he became aware of a horrible cold tingling sensation all over, and the feeling that his hair was standing 'on end'. At this point, he saw a large dog, probably black, come walking through the fence of the big private house known as 'The Elms' on his right, cross the road in front of him, a few feet away, and disappear through the WALL of the Rectory opposite...he found there was no sign whatsoever of any footprints, or other marks on the fresh snow. At this point he panicked and ran fast as he could to my Granny's house in the main street ... At that time my father had no knowledge whatsoever of local ghosts, Bungay Black Dogs etc. ..."

As so often happens in stories of paranormal encounters, the witness first becomes aware that something is "off" when he has a strange sensation in his body. Most readers will recognize, for example, the intense feeling of being watched. We see this so often throughout the wide range of the paranormal, Fortean and cryptozoological that we begin to wonder if humans don't possess an internal sensor or psychic awareness of the strange. Perhaps, our ancestors developed psi in a time when the species had to be more careful of the things that hunt the night, both natural and Otherworldly.

Note, too, that the tale has the Black Dog disappearing into a wall. It seems that this phantom is quite partial to using trees, walls, hedges and fences as locations where it can vanish.

We find this interesting account of a church-related Black Dog on the *Shuckland* website.

This tale occurs in Winterton, Norfolk, in July 2005. Ian Barclay, his sister, her husband, and their ten-year-old twins decided to visit the local church: Holy Trinity and All Saints. Mr. Barclay was told by his sister and her spouse that they had just seen the "biggest, black dog" that they had ever seen run into an elder bush at the corner of the church.

Mr. Barclay assumed that their visitor was simply the local Newfoundland, so he and one of the twin girls thrust their hands into the bush, expecting a large dog to run out. Instead, five blackbirds took wing. The determined fellow penetrated farther into the bush and found nothing resembling a large dog.

Pictures of the church show that, if a large animal of any kind had gone into the bush, the group should have seen it come out.

Mr. Barclay's sister described the animal as "black, with the shape and coat of a retriever. It was the size of a Newfoundland but was not so shaggy and did not have the heavy build".

The postscript to this report is that Mr. Barclay's father went into hospital later that day and died three weeks later, so we may file this apparition securely with our death-omen Dogs as well as haunting a churchyard.

I might even be tempted to wonder if the Black Dog displayed a propensity for shape-shifting, given the presence of the blackbirds. The reader will see later on that the Black Dogs of some regions are said to have more than one form, but I will note that I encountered no Black Dogs that turned to birds in my research other than this one possible account.

A similar story comes to us from Nick Redfern in *The Monster Book*; however, there are no blackbirds in this account.

According to Redfern, the Bradley family was having a stroll around the grounds of the cathedral in Lichfield, Staffordshire, a building that Redfern states is notable for its three spires. The weather was pleasant, but the family had quite a start when they spotted a Black Dog running at high speed along the side of the cathedral.

There was no mistaking the apparition, as it was "the size of a donkey", and as the astonished family looked on, the creature "charged the wall" of the cathedral and, like Constable Stonehouse's Dog, who will appear in a moment, this Black Dog vanished into the stonework of the massive building. The family, at this point, experienced the extreme fear reaction that we see so often in Black Dog sightings and decided to make themselves scarce.

Lichfield Cathedral is the burial site of a number of notable historical people. It would be interesting to know if this Black

Dog ran into a wall adjacent to one of these crypts and, if so, which one.

Mark Norman tells several church/cemetery stories in his book on Black Dog lore.

Norman quotes a story by Grey Usher from the October 1973 issue of *Fate* magazine of a dog that seemed quite ordinary ... until it was not.

Usher was an amateur archeologist, and he was in the habit of picking through newly dug graves for evidence of Roman pottery in his area. He stopped in a country churchyard to pursue his hobby but noted what he took to be the vicar's black dog outside on a porch. Usher, being fond of canines, approached the animal, a "large, smooth haired" animal, but it rose, yawned and disappeared into the porch.

The amateur archeologist decided that this must be a sign that the vicar was at home, so he approached to introduce himself. He followed the dog into the porch and found, to his dismay, that the church was locked tight, and the dog was nowhere to be seen. Usher states that, "I had been only a few yards away when he [the dog] went into the porch and he certainly had not come out again."

The witness, perhaps wisely, decided that he had been warned off his pursuit by the Church Grim and took his hobby elsewhere. I would note that, in the necromantic workings of folk magic traditions like Southern Conjure, taking something from a grave without leaving something in return is very bad form. In fact, before entering a graveyard for magical purposes, some traditions require that you leave an offering for the guardian spirit of the place. One wonders if this fellow simply violated that rule one too many times, and the Black Dog appeared to remind him of his manners.

I also note with interest the mention of the Dog yawning at this witness. We will see several stories where great emphasis is laid on the mouth, tongue or teeth of the Dog in the witness' memory. I am intrigued by this little detail because there is no mention in the legends about why this should be so.

Witnesses to high strangeness events are often viewed by critics as the weak link in any story since most people are not trained observers. Therefore, when one sees a story from law enforcement, one tends to pay special attention.

Mark Norman quotes from a publication by Philip R. Leece about a police constable who spotted a Black Dog while on patrol:

> Police Constable Stonehouse was on duty early one moonlit morning and was riding his bike towards Mow Cop church when "I suddenly became aware of the sounds of an animal panting and running hard towards me, as it seemed from the lower slopes of Mow Cop, when I saw a huge dog jump from the hillside with coal black skin and red eyes, its tongue hanging out and in obvious signs of distress". He told how it ran into the churchyard, and he felt only amazement, not fear, at the sight of this animal. However when he reached the churchyard and saw that the iron gates were locked, he realised that the animal, which clearly had seemed to be a real one, must have gone through the gates and was therefore a ghost.

I found myself wondering why the constable did not suspect something was amiss when he noted that the dog had red eyes. Also, it is interesting to note that the constable felt no fear during this encounter despite the creepy circumstances, but only amazement. As we have seen throughout the reading so far, witness reactions tend to trend toward terror, but, like UFO witnesses, one can't be certain how one will react in the presence of a Black Dog until the event occurs.

The other question mark that appears in my mind related to

this account is: why was the Dog so obviously distressed? The apparition does not appear to pay any mind to the constable, so one would assume that he was not the cause of its apparent anxiety. Perhaps this graveyard Black Dog was dealing with an issue outside the realms of normal human perception?

Norman has two other stories that pertain to churches and cemeteries, both of which involve memorial markers.

In the first account, a man who later wrote books about the sea who was living at Chideock, in the county of Dorset, before World War II, was walking home one night when he and his companion were shadowed by a "large, black animal which padded along beside us, all the way". The future author noted that the whole experience was uncanny but became "a great deal more uncanny when, as we reached the old graveyard at the crossroads (to North Chideock and Seaton) we stood silent and watched the hound pad its way towards an enormous gravestone and disappear before our eyes".

The witness notes that the moon provided him with plenty of light. An investigator looking at this case might have been interested in who was buried under that huge monument and whether there were any interesting local legends attached to that person.

The above is an example of a more or less modern marker story, but there is also a Black Dog associated with a set of much older markers. In the Quantock Hills, county of Somerset, one may find cairns. These man-made piles of stone are used in many regions for several purposes, but according to online sources for the area, the cairns have been recognized as prehistoric funerary monuments.

Those ancient burial sites appear to have a Black Dog associated with them, at least according to another Norman story. Around 1957, a hunter returning from a stag hunt on horseback came across a large black dog that caused his horse to "swerve and gallop" such that the equine had to be urged back to a walk. The horse was terrified by this dog, and the rider reports that he, too, broke into a cold sweat at the presence of this anomalous beast. The hunter states that "the dog seemed to come from one cairn and follow along to disappear into another one".

This Black Dog must have been quite impressive to so terrorize a man who was, undoubtedly, well armed. While we will discuss ley lines later in the book, it would seem that this phantom was following a straight track from one cairn to another.

The final story of this section on churchyards, cemeteries and other burial sites is from the files of Simon Sherwood. This is a relatively modern account from April 2005, and it takes place in the region of Brackley in Northamptonshire:

> Until last night I had never heard of this phenomenon ... The time was 10pm. I left the house to make a phone call on my mobile due to receiving no phone signal inside ... As I walked towards St Peter's church yard I regained the signal and so strolled through the gates and along the path of the south graveyard towards the church. After walking only a few metres along the path I heard a loud panting and galloping of feet in front of me. I wasn't sure what was coming but didn't have time to think as within seconds [a] large black shaggy dog was running towards me. It appeared frantic and ran incredibly quickly. It was dark and so it was hard to tell but it either had large flapping ears or horns upon its head. It's [sic] eyes were ... black and glinting in the light. It ran right up to me, within inches and then was enveloped in darkness and faded away. I was naturally very scared and had a very sleepless night.

While this individual was on foot, this story reminds me of any number of tales that we will see later where a Black Dog seems bound to collide with a vehicle and then disappears just before impact. I found it interesting that the witness described the Black Dog as "frantic". Although this description is seen in other places, it is not the norm, and one wonders what might have upset this Dog so. The use of an electronic device in the graveyard or some Otherworldy issue that most humans could not see?

The Phantom Black Dogs that inhabit churchyards, cemeteries and other burial sites are just as mysterious as the apparitions with larger territories. As noted in the History section of the book, dogs in general, and especially Black Dogs, have been associated with the dead and the land of the dead since humans began recording history.

While it is evident that the Black Dog, with its strong links to death, which will be explored in a later chapter, has a place in these funerary locales, one still wonders what the Dog's purpose is for such haunts. Excepting the Demon Dog of Valle Crucis, most of the phantoms in this section have seemed relatively harmless. If it truly is their purpose to guard these sites, one would think that more of these sightings would fall into the aggressive category.

Once more, the Black Dog refuses to be easily filed into a ready-made pigeonhole.

While the vast majority of these apparitions are seen outdoors, there is a small subset of Phantom Black Dogs, like Linda Godfrey's Manwolf, that are seen indoors, often in witness' bedrooms. The next chapter will examine some of these accounts.

7

HOME SWEET HOME

WHILE IT IS QUITE one thing for the Phantom Black Dog to haunt roads or rivers or even cemeteries, it is quite another thing to find this being inside one's home; nevertheless, that is exactly what is reported in a certain number of Black Dog cases.

First, it should be noted that these accounts take place inside the walls of a home, not on the grounds. Legend notes that the Black Dog sometimes attaches itself to a family and, indeed, such a case will be discussed in the chapter on the Dog as a death omen. It would be natural for a Black Dog associated with a family to be seen on the grounds of that family's home or manor. These are not the accounts discussed in this section. In the accounts of this chapter, there is a Black Dog seen inside a home, and in at least one case, the apparition has an actual, physical and deadly effect.

Janet and Colin Bord, in *Alien Animals*, relate an account that came to them in personal correspondence. The percipient was a child during World War II and took refuge from the relentless bombing of the cities in a cottage at Bredon, Worcestershire. The witness was sitting up in their bed one evening when a Black Dog suddenly appeared in the room. This creature must have been massive, as the teller of the tale stated that they were sitting on an old-fashioned bed frame, and the creature was as tall as the bedstead and displayed the characteristic fiery red eyes.

The witness perceived that the Black Dog was looking her in the eyes when it vanished without a trace.

A particularly impressive aspect of this story was this witness' repeated statement that she was sure she was not asleep. She demonstrates this fact by recalling the exact bird-calls audible in the room and other noises from the neighbour-hood. As well, we should note that the witness plainly states that she was sitting up. While it is possible to doze off while sitting up, as soon as the person enters sleep and the body relaxes, the individual will fall over. There is no note of this in the witness' statement.

Personally, I think that the skeptical assumption that someone sitting in bed must be dreaming is ridiculous. I would submit that a number of people reading this book are doing so in their beds. I would hope that my readers are not asleep or falling asleep.

Mark Norman gives us the account of Mrs. Garth-Heyworth of Crosscombe Manor from a personal letter dated 1960.

The witness was getting ready to receive guests and was working on altering some curtains when she happened to glance up and see a "big black hound (like a staghound) rush through the door and upstairs". Mrs. Garth-Heyworth had a mixed-breed sighthound named Psyche and feared that the dog had gotten into the house and was placing muddy paws on the newly laundered linens.

The witness called out for her husband and gave chase, mounting the stairs and climbing to the top floor of the house. There was no sign of the dog anywhere, and she went back downstairs to speak with her husband. He wanted to know what all the fuss was about, as Psyche was asleep in her kennel on the other side of the house.

One might imagine that the witness had somehow made a mistake except that she saw this animal on the grounds of the house later, "running round the lily pond in the garden and I watched from my bedroom window and saw it take a twelve-foot jump over a high bush hedge and vanish in the jump ..."

A staghound is not a recognized breed but a hybrid hunting dog that looks a great deal like a Scottish deerhound, a less massive version of the Irish wolfhound. All the dogs in this class are tall and sturdy, so seeing one in one's house, particularly a pure black one, would be startling.

While nothing in the appearance and behaviour of the animal in the house indicates anything but a normal dog, and it's certainly possible that a physical dog could have gotten into the house and then out without being seen, the coincidence of such an event is striking. What are the odds that another staghound, an uncommon breed, much less a pure black one, an uncommon colour, would appear in this home?

We also have to bear in mind the witness' later sighting of a similar animal on the grounds of the estate. Its athletic proclivities alone take it into the Otherworldly realms.

While on the subject of manor houses and halls, the Black Dog of Blickling Hall can be discussed. Now, this story seems more legend than witness account, but it is interesting nonetheless and comes from Enid Porter's article "Fairies, Ghosts and Black Dogs".

In the tale, Lord and Lady Lothian are having some partitions destroyed in the hall to make space for a dining room. An old woman of the village tells a clergyman that this is a big mistake, and when he asks why, she tells him that the Black Dog will return to run the house.

According to her story, a certain fellow went fishing one day in the local lake and caught an enormous fish. Once he landed the fish, an equally enormous Black Dog came out of its mouth and ran circles in the hall until a "wise man" came from London and settled the Dog by installing the partitions. The old woman was very concerned since, if they let the Dog loose again, there were no more "wise men" in London who could "lay" the thing.

This type of story is more typical of the tales we hear of the faery, where a half dozen incredible things happen before breakfast, but it is quite difficult to ignore. I would love to know if the Lothians had any issues after knocking the partitions down and why this Black Dog, of all Black Dogs, emerged from the belly of a fish, a completely unique feature of this tale.

This story bears a close resemblance to those told of what folklorists class as the trooping fairies. This species of the fae travel from place to place, often using the straight tracks or paths of their own, and folk wisdom was that building a home on one of these paths was a recipe for trouble.

In the case of this Black Dog, the movement was stopped (or perhaps rerouted) by the partitions. For the fae, someone unfortunate enough to live on one of these paths might have to leave their doors and windows open at certain periods to allow the travellers to troop through without obstruction.

Simon Sherwood, an academic who studies anomalous experiences, states that his interest in the paranormal came from his own experience of a Black Dog as a child. The tale, detailed in his article "Black Dogs of England", is as follows:

> The year was about 1974. I had been in bed a couple of hours. I awoke to hear a patter of feet. I looked up thinking it was my dog, but to my terror I saw a massive black animal probably with horns but perhaps ears, galloping along the landing towards my bedroom. I tried to scream but I found it impossible. The creatures [sic] eyes were bright yellow and as

big as saucers. The animal got to my bedroom door and then vanished as quick as it had appeared.

I believed this [my parents' explanation for my experience] until a few years later when I was reading a local paper which had an article about a haunted council house which was inhabited by a poltergeist. A variety of objects were hurled at the family's baby child. The father claimed that a black dog rushed at him and then disappeared. He also claimed that a black goat had been seen running around the house ... After reading this article I was convinced that what I thought had happened a few years back had most probably happened.

Interestingly, in all of the above stories, the Black Dog appears and disappears within the immediate confines of the home. The apparition does not, for example, appear in someone's bedroom and then run through a wall to vanish. Instead, it is almost as if the Black Dog is confined to one space. I found myself wondering, after reading the Blickling Hall tale, whether the walls of the rooms prevented the Dog from wandering.

As the book continues, one will see, again and again, examples of Black Dogs seeming to haunt a certain territory – a stretch of road, a body of water, a cemetery and so on. This fact naturally gives rise to the question: why would a Black Dog be in someone's house? One wonders if it might not be the case that the house was constructed over a section of the Black Dog's territory.

In *Alien Animals*, the Bords spend some time discussing ley line theory in their section on Black Dogs. They speak of the work of Alfred Watkins, who theorized that many of the sacred sites and archeological wonders of Britain, such as Stonehenge and Glastonbury Tor, are aligned along long "straight tracks".

Theorists also feel that the Earth's energies are aligned along these lines. A close friend of mine who has since passed explained ley lines to me as the energy grid of the planet, somewhat similar to the meridian system of traditional Chinese medicine, a system of energy lines in the human body that can be manipulated to improve health. The sacred sites would be analogous to the points that Chinese medicine practitioners use to improve a client's well-being.

If one is seeing Black Dogs in one's home, might it not be that the house is parked on one of these ley lines or even at a key line juncture?

While the vast majority of Black Dog stories do not end in anyone or anything being directly harmed, the story of Pierre van Paassen takes another tack entirely.

Van Paassen was a journalist who had a long career as a foreign correspondent, and in the spring of 1929, the journalist was renting a private home in Bourg-en-Foret, France. Van Paassen had occasion to see a large Black Dog pass him on the stairs and then disappear when it reached the landing. As with all good ghost stories, the man made a thorough search of the home, to no avail.

Van Paassen did not mention the sighting to anyone, but after being away from home for a trip, he returned to find that several others had encountered the Black Dog. The journalist, being, apparently, the curious sort, decided to stay up with a neighbour and his young son to see if the Black Dog would appear.

The creature did appear and seemed friendly as the trio mounted the stairs to get a better look, but as so often happens in these tales, the dog faded from sight as they climbed the stairs.

A few days later, Van Paassen decided to watch for the Dog again, but he made a pivotal error. He brought along his two "police dogs" (possibly German shepherds). The Black Dog materialized and made its way partly down the stairs before it vanished again. The police dogs apparently engaged their invisible adversary:

> This led to a horrible scene. The dogs pricked up their ears at the first noise on the floor above and leaped for the door. The sound of pattering feet was coming downstairs as usual, but I saw nothing. What my dogs saw I do not know, but their hair stood on end and they retreated growling back into my room, baring their fangs and snarling. Presently they howled as if they were in excruciating pain and were snapping and biting in all directions, as if they were fighting some fierce enemy. I had never seen them in such mortal panic. I could not come to their aid, for I saw nothing to strike with the cudgel I held in my hand. Then one of my dogs yelled as if he were in his death-throes, fell on the floor and died ...

Being a dog lover, I found this story horrific, but it does fall into place amongst stories where the Black Dog will retaliate if molested, and this Dog seems particularly aggressive, as Van Paassen notes that the dogs were retreating, a common sign of a paranormal event.

No external signs of injury were found on the police dog, but its death was the last straw. Van Paassen decided to seek help from a local priest.

In a strange postscript, the priest is summoned, and that individual laid the blame for the apparition on one of the house servants, a young girl, stating mysteriously that there was sometimes an "affinity" between young people and the paranormal. The poor child was dismissed, and the sightings stopped.

There is so much to this story that one could probably write a book about it. Young people and particularly young women are often said to be the focus of poltergeist activity. One of the problems with the folkloric studies of the Black Dog is that one often has no idea how old the storytellers are.

It is possible and, indeed, probable that some young people encountered Black Dogs, but this hardly seems sufficient to attach the phenomenon to their agency. One suspects that the Abbé in this story knew something that he was not telling the house occupants and their landlord, either about the servant girl or the house itself.

Is it possible that the girl was somehow creating the apparition? We will explore such possibilities in the Theories section of this work.

In our travels so far, we have been through the UK, US and Canada. We have one other location to visit, the area south of the US border, where tales of the Black Dog take a somewhat different turn.

8

SOUTH OF THE (US) BORDER

AFTER SOME CONSIDERATION, this writer decided that the Phantom Black Dog, as it manifests in the Latin American areas south of the US border, deserves a section all its own.

This part of the book would be impossible without the work of Simon Burchell in his monographs *Phantom Black Dogs in Latin America* and *Phantom Black Dogs in Pre-Hispanic Mexico*, both of which are freely available online. Mr. Burchell's fluency in Spanish and time in Guatemala allowed him to do research in these areas and provide us with some interesting accounts of the Black Dog phenomenon in an entirely different cultural milieu and in an area with a living tradition of both shamanism and witchcraft.

Latin America, in this volume, will refer to all the lands south of the US border from Mexico through Central America and into South America. As in Britain, the Black Dog has a number of different names in the various countries of Latin America. In Mexico, the Dog might be called a Nahual or Huay Chivo, although these names also refer to a species of sorcerer that is said to shape-shift into animal forms. Those forms include a Black Dog, and these sorcerers might be likened to

Skinwalkers in the North American indigenous traditions, though not with the reputation for murder and cannibalism that Skinwalkers have acquired.

In most of Central America, for example Honduras, Nicaragua, El Salvador and Panama, the Black Dog is known as the Cadejo. In South America, in Colombia, the Dog is called Carbunco; in Ecuador, Allcusacra; in Argentina, it may be the Familiar or the Lobisón, although a Lobisón seems to be more of a werewolf than a Black Dog. In many places, the phantom is simply referred to by its Spanish name, Perro Negro, Black Dog.

Interestingly, in his book *Phantom Black Dogs in Pre-Hispanic Mexico*, Burchell lays out a case for the very early association of the Black Dog with Tezcatlipoca, an interesting and multifaceted Aztec god, based on the 1529 writings of Bernardino de Sahagún.

This Franciscan friar wrote a critically important work called *Historia General de las cosas de Nueva España* [General History of the Things of New Spain], a "monumental catalogue of Aztec beliefs and customs and the natural history of central Mexico. In his effort to acquaint Spaniards with the beliefs and customs of the Aztecs so that the culture could be snuffed out, Sahagún provided historians with invaluable insight into those pre-colonial beliefs". In the book, the friar notes the following:

> ... they said that Tezcatlipoca often transformed himself into an animal that they call cóyutl [i.e. coyote – SB], that is like a wolf. And thus transformed it would place itself in the path of travellers, blocking their path so they could not continue. And in this the traveller understood that some danger of thieves or robbers lay ahead, or that some other misfortune would occur upon the road ahead.

The god, in this dog-like form, is seen to act in a manner

very consistent with the Phantom Black Dog accounts of Britain. Particularly note that the god was said to protect travelers by blocking their way as they journeyed along a road. This is behaviour that we have seen in the Black Dog already and will see again.

Because Tezcatlipoca was the embodiment of "the forces of fate, night, darkness, violent storms and ... crossroads", he, of all the gods of the Aztecs, was singled out as the manifestation of the Christian Devil in Aztec form, and thus, Burchell theorizes, these dog-like manifestation were intimately associated with the Devil early on in the minds of the Spanish colonizers.

That association continues to the modern day though it seems to have softened somewhat in the unusual belief that there are two types of spectral dog, a black one and a white one. The Black Dog is a malevolent spirit that seems to attach itself particularly to alcoholics, while the White Dog is a protective spirit that is often viewed as a manifestation of the witness' guardian angel.

A good example of the White Dog is found in this account of a schoolteacher that Burchell translated from folklorist Lara Figueroa:

Ángel Flores, a school teacher studying law in Guatemala City told Lara Figueroa of a man named Juan Carlos who lived in a shack in the south of the city in the area now occupied by the airport and the zoo. Juan Carlos was often working away from home until quite late. When he returned from work, without fail he used to find a white dog opposite his front door. When it saw him, it used to circle behind the shack and vanish without trace. He was told that this was the white Cadejo that protected his wife and children while he was working.

White dogs, in the British lore, are related to the faery (Cu

Sith) so there is some divergence here between Hispanic and Anglo folklore of the Black Dog. It seems that the British, rather than seeing Dogs of a different colour, simply decided that there were malevolent and benevolent Black Dogs and left the matter at that.

It is also worth noting, while looking at the possible pre-Hispanic origins of the Black Dog in Mexico and farther south, that the Aztecs, particularly, had a strong belief that dogs were psychopomps, that is that they actually carried the souls of the departed into the land of the dead, and without them, there was no way to cross the "wide, deep river" that separated those souls from their final destination. This belief was so prevalent that, in some periods, dogs were cremated with their owners to provide this service.

Burchell goes on to give the following personal information that brings such beliefs into the present day:

Interestingly, my Guatemalan wife assures me that the local Maya near Quetzaltenango, Guatemala's second city, believe that dogs should not be mistreated because the dead need the help of a dog to cross a river in the afterlife, and that if a person mistreats a dog that help will not be forthcoming. One local shaman told her that the newly deceased needs to grip the tail of the dog as it swims across the river in order to cross.

The section on history earlier in the book points out the association of dogs with death in other regions and how those dogs of legend and their association with the dead and the land of the dead may have contributed to the Black Dog legends of today. It seems that the same process may have occurred in the Latin American lands.

While much of the Black Dog mythos in Latin America is similar to what is seen in, for example, the United Kingdom, there is one aspect of the accounts that seems to derive from the living tradition of shamanism and witchcraft mentioned earlier. There are a number of accounts where the saucer-eyed Black Dog is actually a sorcerer, what in Mexico is called a Nahual or a Huay Chivo.

An excellent and amusing story of this type is the tale of the smoking Black Dog. Burchell says the following about this account:

> Trawling the Spanish language newspapers on the Internet, although tedious, can occasionally throw up some interesting results. On 1 March 2006, the Mexican local newspaper *Diario de Yucatán* reported a frightening encounter during a period of paranoia about the activities of an unidentified sorcerer. Mr. Dzib Pech was with his wife, María Luciana Tuz Aceo, on his motorcycle returning home to Tizimín after visiting their parents in Pocoboch, in Yucatán state in the southeast of the country. It was 8.30 in the evening and they were just coming up to the junction with the Valladolid-Tizimín main road when Dzib Pech noticed something beside the road. He shone the light of his motorbike on it to reveal a black dog, hunched over at the side of the road and smoking a cigarette!
>
> It appeared to hurl itself at them but faded away, giving them the fright of their lives. This apparition was attributed to the activities of the huay chivo, a shape-shifting Maya sorcerer (huay or wáay in Yucatec Maya) ...

While the idea of a Black Dog having a smoke on the side of the road may bring a smile, it must be remembered that the Huay Chivo is deadly serious business to the people of this area, and such sorcerers were said to use their shape-shifting powers to attain greater wealth by stealing from others.

Burchell provides a good account of this in the stories of the related Nahual, another species of shape-shifting magic user that often took the form of a Black Dog. Burchell spoke with a witness who gave him the account of a group of Mexican peasants who, when faced with the mysterious loss of livestock in their area, mounted a guard on the animal pens.

Two young men monitoring the pens, rifles in hand, felt an "eerie presence" in the early morning hours and discovered an enormous animal, "neither a dog nor a coyote" with red eyes hovering so close to them that they could smell its foul breath. Although the two were justifiably frightened, one youth managed to grab his rifle and shoot at the beast. He missed, but the two then raised the alarm only to discover that the creature was gone.

The village populace consulted another sorcerer (It takes a Nahual to catch a Nahual? Or was this, perhaps, another sort of folk magician?), and he confirmed that the animal was not a natural beast and prescribed steps for trapping it. The peasants followed those steps carefully and, on the second night, were able to shoot and kill the animal. Though they still could not say what the thing was, they hung the corpse from a tree and went to bed.

In the morning, they discovered the body of one of the locals, a man who had moved to the area some months earlier but kept to himself. He had been changing into a Black Dog to steal food, an aspect of the sorcerer stories that can also be found in European werewolf lore. Burchell points out the similarity between this tale and some accounts of shape-shifting witches in Europe, where the witch was harmed in his or her animal form and then discovered later via those injuries in their human form. When we talk about magical thought later in the book, we will find an interesting explanation for this phenomenon.

As mentioned previously, Burchell lived in Guatemala and

thus had many stories of the Cadejo from that region in his work. One of these stories will be sufficient to give a flavour for the Cadejo stories and especially their relation to alcohol:

> ... a mule driver who was drinking with his employees in the previously mentioned Cerrito del Carmen area of Guatemala City when he caught one of his workers pretending to drink while secretly pouring the liquor away. The mule driver, named as Ceferino Escobar, furiously reprimanded his subordinate, Tiburcio, who defended himself by claiming that he did not drink because whenever he got drunk he would see the Cadejo.
>
> When his boss mocked him, Tiburcio challenged him to get drunk with him. The two became completely inebriated and staggered off to take a siesta. A short distance from the bar they both passed out beneath a palm tree. Night set in and Tiburcio awoke to hear far off the claws of a dog striking the cobbles, gradually getting closer. At the same time he saw two glowing balls of fire that gradually grew in size as they got nearer. Terrified, he tried to awaken his boss without success. The dogs [*sic*] claws striking the ground now sounded like a goat's hooves. There in front of him "was an animal that looked like a dog with burning eyes, crouched to attack". Terrified and with his head still spinning, he passed out.
>
> The two awoke early the next morning with their clothes torn to rags. They were beneath a tree beside one of the principal streets of the district without knowing how they had gotten there. Both feeling rather ill, they hit another bar to drink away their hangovers, wondering what had happened in the night. When Ceferino counted his mules, one was missing so they both returned to the Cerrito del Carmen to look for it. They found it tied up nearby and a local man told them "You should thank me for finding it. Last night a madman was on

the loose with his machete attacking anyone he could find. They say that he would have killed two people sleeping under a palm tree if it weren't for their dog guarding them". After that, we are told, Ceferino Escobar never mocked his workers' beliefs again ...

Unlike British Black Dog stories, which seem to downplay or deny drunkenness, if it is mentioned at all, the Guatemalan Cadejo stories tend to stress alcohol consumption and the role of the Cadejo in safeguarding the lives of the inebriated.

Lest someone think that the Cadejo assumes this guardian role from good-heartedness, remember that the Cadejo is strongly associated in this predominantly Roman Catholic country with the Devil. The belief is that the Cadejo is guarding the person until the time that they die from their alcoholism. At that point, this species of Black Dog is said to harvest the person's soul.

I find this thinking suspect. If the Cadejo wanted to harvest the souls of drunkards, why would it not simply do it when it came across the person passed out and helpless in some side street? Why would it wait until the person died naturally before dragging them off to the Nether Realms? It seems to me that this is simply an example of the local Church taking advantage of a local legend to discourage drunkenness.

Before turning away from this area of the world, there is one more interesting variant of the Black Dog lore from El Salvador that needs to be mentioned. Salvadoreños believe that if the Cadejo is nearby, its distinctive howl will sound in the distance, while, if the Cadejo is far away, the howl will come from nearby. This is extremely useful information since the Cadejo is known to follow people over long distances, and if a frightened person should be overtaken, they are in trouble.

This habit of following people over long distances is interesting in light of the European Black Dogs territorial ways. What boundaries are present in, for example, the UK that are not present in Latin America?

The Salvadoran Cadejo, unlike its sometimes milder brothers across the sea, does not respond well to attacks. If it is assaulted, it will swell to the size of a bull and trample its unfortunate victim, leaving them "paralysed and struck dumb with terror at the side of the road". Victims do recover, but the process often takes weeks. We will see some incidents, later in the book, where victims of the British Black Dog also ended up unconscious in ditches. While there is no mention of paralysis in these cases, it is noted that the victim is difficult to revive.

This paralysis and loss of speech is but the first of many strange aspects of the folklore of Black Dogs that will be revealed in the next section of the book.

SECTION THREE

ASPECTS OF BLACK DOG FOLKLORE

It is now some years since Dr. Margaret Murray
suggested that I should attempt a survey of
this ubiquitous ghost. The picture is by no
means complete, but it is beginning to
stabilize, and certain patterns are beginning
to emerge that suggest some tentative theories
...

Theo Brown
"The Black Dog"

9

THE WITNESSES

BEFORE MOVING FURTHER into the realms of Phantom Black Dog lore and our explorations of the varied aspects of strangeness attached to that lore, we must consider the people who are reporting these sightings. Both Ethel Rudkin and Theo Brown had strong feelings about the people whom they interviewed and their trustworthiness.

Rudkin admits on the first page of her seminal article that she is a witness herself, and she is very adamant about the people whom she has gotten stories from. She states unequivocally that she never got an account from anyone "who was weak either in mind or body".

Theo Brown defends her percipients by noting that: "There seems no reason why we should doubt them; the dog has been seen by a very mixed crowd of people, mainly country-folk who, as any folklorist knows, are often the most sceptical of mortals, and certainly have no monopoly of superstition ..."

I am inclined to agree with Ms. Brown in her assessment. One of the things that struck me, particularly in reading the older accounts, is the straightforward, matter-of-fact presentation of the tales. The early, seminal sources of Black Dog lore are all folklorists, and it is obvious that they do not see themselves as investigators. Instead, they view their job as preserving the stories and folklore of the region they are interested in.

So if the farmer down the road tells a folklorist that he saw the Phantom Black Dog when he was a young man and it happened at such and such a location and the Dog looked thus, then that is exactly what a folklorist will record.

While a modern-day investigator might dig at the witness for a better description of the beast, more detail on the location, more context on the sighting, the witness' feelings during the sighting, etc., the folklorist simply records what they are told, often word for word, trying to get as much of the story and its flavour as possible, and then moves on.

This lack of follow-up might give the modern investigator heartburn, but given the terror that a Black Dog sighting can engender, it is fortunate that these stories were preserved at all.

While it is true that quite a number of people viewed the Dog as harmless (some tried to pet it) or even beneficent (as we will see in the guardian stories later), we often hear of witnesses with the same reaction as this farmer in Dahlgren's *South Mountain Magic*:

> He saw the Black Dog stalking down the hillside path, and as he stopped to look at him he had the sensation "that the hill was coming down on him", which almost paralyzed his faculties, so benumbed did he feel – "My nervous system was racked to the centre," the man said, in telling his story! Of course, everyone knows, when a man's nerves are shaken, that it means something very dreadful ...

Dahlgren goes on to make some rather sexist remarks about the difference between men and women taking fright, but the point is made. The people she was writing about were tough, pioneer types who, in other stories from the book, tried to fight the Black Dog or put a bullet in it. These were tough-minded people with no reason to make up foolish stories and, one would imagine, might be reluctant to mention that something shook their nerves under more normal circumstances.

If a Black Dog can produce this sort of fear in hardy country folk on both sides of the ocean, then we are fortunate that the folklorists were able to overcome the reticence of their witnesses and collect the many stories that they did.

The conclusion to the book will contain some other thoughts about witnesses, but there we have a long journey before we get to those closing thoughts. The Phantom Black Dog is associated with all manner of high strangeness and, in this section of the book, some of the weird aspects of the Black Dog stories will be explored. Many of these phenomena have been frequently ascribed to the Dog, but I will begin with items that are noted but not as often found in the lore.

10

STORMS?

THERE ARE legends that associate the Black Dog with storms, but the research shows a dearth of stories that support this claim. The Bords, in their book *Alien Animals*, have the following to say about this issue:

> In traditional lore the black dog also appears as a forecaster of bad weather. The appearance of Le Tchan de Bouôlé (the dog of Bouley) usually presaged a storm in Jersey, and when the Black Shuck was seen on the road between Aldeburgh and Cromer on the East Anglian coast it was nearly always before bad weather. It is interesting to note in this connection that the black dog which wreaked such havoc in Bungay and Blythburgh churches in 1577 did so during a terrible thunderstorm ...

Given that the Bungay story is one of the first recorded stories of a Black Dog and the emphasis that Fleming gives to the storm in his tract describing those events, I would think that the "traditional lore" might simply have come from this old legend that irrevocably ties the Black Dog to a massive storm.

There are several witness accounts in this book that relate to storms such as the 1972 sighting of a Black Dog on Gorleston Beach by Coastguard Graham Grant. This story is detailed in chapter 5, but it should be noted that, in the postscript to that story, it is mentioned that a gale blew in shortly after this witness had his encounter.

Additionally, in chapter 14, we will find the story of Adam, the unfortunate recipient of a death portent from a Black Dog that appeared to him during a sudden snowstorm. In the story of S. Costea, that also appears in a later chapter, the witness noted that the Black Dog haunting their home site preyed on their chickens and rabbits "after thunderstorms".

When we move to the series of stories about Random Oddities that appear at the end of this section of the book, we see several accounts that relate to storms. The World War II tale of an airman and his wife who had a Black Dog banging on the sides of their house takes place on a "stormy evening". In Norfolk, we encounter the tale of a mother trying to buy milk on a "thundery evening" whose son claimed that a Black Dog tried to enter the vehicle while she was gone. Finally, we have the story of Ron Palfrey of Palm Springs where Palfrey sighted two Black Dogs on a rainy night in the desert.

Having lived in the Arizona desert, I checked to see if Palm Springs has a "monsoon season", and it does. These desert storm seasons are characterized by short, fierce storms that may contain high winds and copious lightning and thunder, so I think we have to posit a storm link in this story as well.

I am still of the opinion that the Black Dog storm link comes more from the legendary encounter of the Black Dog of Bungay with its monstrous storm in progress, seemingly setting the scene for a supernatural incursion. The fact remains that many Black Dog tales note the weather as clear and even tell us that the moon was out and bright. Then we have the accounts I have summarized above where a Black Dog appears in conjunction with a storm. Given that fair weather seems more common than foul weather in the Black Dog lore, I am of the opinion that we need to leave the assertion of a link between Black Dogs and storms open for further investigation and research.

11

HAVING A CHAT

WHILE THE VAST majority of Phantom Black Dog stories feature an animal apparition that is either completely silent or that makes sounds one would associate with a dog, such as barking, howling, growling or panting, there are a couple of stories in the annals where the Dog actually speaks to someone.

As one might expect, the first of these stories comes from Ethel Rudkin.

In this account, a monthly nurse, a provider who specialized in assisting women during their "lying in" period after child-birth, was needed at a farm near Belle Hole, Lincolnshire. While she was there, the other children were talking of the boggart, a local name for the Black Dog, and asked what the nurse would do should she encounter the creature. She replied, one assumes in jest, that she would put it in her pocket.

As the nurse made her way home to Kirton that evening, after the sun had set, a Black Dog appeared and circled her, saying repeatedly, "Put me in your pocket, put me in your pocket ..."

There is no record of the poor nurse's reaction, but it should be noted that a boggart, in folklore, can also be a faery being that does not seem to be confined to a single shape. Thus, this story may not be dealing with a "true" Black Dog, as the boggart is known to be mischievous, and the "put me in your pocket" story sounds like exactly the sort of nonsense a mischievous faery might get up to.

The other talking Black Dog account comes from Ivan Bunn and the newsletter *Lantern*. As it is a short account, I will quote it in its entirety:

> Last century a former dweller in Clopton Green, Sufflok [*sic*], saw a "thing" with two saucer eyes, on the road to Woolpit the night before he died. It would not move out of the way and grew bigger and bigger and it said, "I shall be wanting you within the week.'

Again, such speech is entirely uncharacteristic and, given the man's demise shortly after the sighting, one is left to wonder what more there might be to this story. I find it telling that the apparition is described as a "thing" and not specifically named as a Black Dog. The saucer eyes do give some credence to the assumption that this is our subject, but I would say that the matter is certainly not settled.

Given that these are the only two stories of a talking Black Dog encountered in the research for this book and that the identity of these two speaking apparitions is in some doubt, I am not convinced that the Phantom Black Dog is at all loquacious. If the reader should encounter a talking specimen, I would love to hear about it.

We have one other uncommon association with the Black Dog that takes us for a guest appearance in another Fortean area: UFOs.

12

LOOK, UP IN THE SKY!

THE STRANGENESS that surrounds the Phantom Black Dog is already evident in the tales that we have reviewed so far. As this section progresses, the reader will encounter invisible Black Dogs, see Dogs that are impervious to firearms and other forms of physical harm, wonder at the seeming ability of some Black Dogs to change shape, and even wander across a Dog or two that decides to walk on its hind legs.

Before moving into those tales, the work of Janet and Colin Bord in *Alien Animals* brings another layer of strangeness to the attention of the researcher. The Bords point out several stories where our erstwhile hounds are seen in the company of another great mystery, the UFO.

Author's note: I have been interested in the UFO phenomenon since I heard my father's sighting story as a child. While I know that the current trend is to use the initials UAP (unidentified aerial phenomena), I am old school about my flying saucers and will continue to use the initials UFO for unidentified flying object. Please forgive the stubbornness of a child of the sixties who cut his UFO research teeth on books like John G. Fuller's

Incident at Exeter and Frank Edwards' *Flying Saucers: Serious Business.*

The first story on our docket is one where an exception has been made to the "no dogs of another colour" rule. The account is so strange that I felt compelled to include it in this compilation of UFO accounts.

The witness had already had a UFO sighting, and this figures compellingly into the story. On 23 August 1977, the woman was awakened at 0225 hours by knocking on her front door. She rose, went to the door and opened it. There stood a huge, white dog that stared at her. We will discuss the intense regard of the Black Dog shortly.

Most persons would have been quite curious about this dog. Where did it come from? Had a person come to visit, bringing the dog along? Why on earth is this dog staring at me in the middle of the night?

Instead, the witness seems to have had one of the uncharacteristic reactions that seem to accompany high strangeness. She closed the door and returned to her bed.

The knocks sounded again, and, again, the woman arose, went to the door and opened it. There was nothing there, not even a large white dog. The woman went back upstairs and turned off the lights, this time waiting by an open window. When she heard pounding on her door again, she poked her head out the window.

Again, nothing was there, but the next day, there was a report of a UFO sighted over the town where the woman lived.

In some of John Keel's work, the percipients had poltergeist-type phenomenon in synchrony with UFOs in their area and, later in this work, a Black Dog will allegedly keep a couple awake all night by banging on the walls of their cottage. Additionally, Sasquatch is often accused of being a wall banger, even though the Hairy One may or may not be seen during these events. The incessant knocking on the door seems to be in line with incidents of high strangeness but is not specific to Black Dog behaviour.

On the subject of UFOs specifically, the large white dog that stared at the witness could also have been what UFO researchers and psychologists call a screen memory. Without going into technical detail, a screen memory is usually a visual memory that covers over a traumatic memory. In UFO research, screen memories are thought to cover close encounters with the occupants of the UFO.

For readers interested in screen memories and UFO encounters, I recommend Mike Clelland's, *The Messengers*, which covers this phenomenon in great and haunting detail. Clelland focuses on owls as a possible screen memory but mentions that people have seen deer and other animals as screens for the beings of a close encounter.

We do not know if this witness experienced any missing time, another hallmark of UFO contact, but, given the general weirdness of this sequence of events, we cannot ignore the possibility that the witness had a close encounter. Whether that encounter was with so-called aliens (I am not a great believer in the extraterrestrial hypothesis) or a white version of the Black Dog is difficult to discern.

The other story that the Bords bring forward for their readers happened in South Africa on 14 December 1963, and in this account, the Black Dog and the UFO are seen in much closer proximity.

As so often happens with these accounts, two men are driving in the wee hours of the morning along the Potchefstroom to Vereeniging Road, just south of Johannesburg. They saw an animal in the road that they, at first, mistook for a buck, and they turned around to investigate. What they found was something that "appeared to be an exceptionally large dog".

Again, there is an odd reaction to the sighting. The two men see this huge dog and simply turn their car around to continue their journey. There is no indication of panicked flight in the account; the two seemed not to have been strongly affected at all.

The night was about to get stranger, however. As they were turning about, the area was brightly illuminated and:

> ... a strange bright object appeared ahead of us and made straight for our car at a terrific speed. I was afraid that the object would hit our car, so I jumped out absolutely petrified. Mr. Muller did likewise. Standing next to the car in the tarred road, we were astounded to see the object dive right over our car and ascend up into the sky ...

The object made several passes at the car and the astonished men before finally racing off to whatever other assignations it had that night.

UFOs are not my primary area of research, but I am not seeing a clear link between our subject and the UFO phenomenon in either of these tales.

The dog in the first story was white, not black, and did not have the glowing red eyes so common to our subject. Also, I can think of no other account where a Black Dog appears on someone's doorstep. Additionally, the witness had already reported a UFO encounter, and the UFO phenomenon seems to enjoy serial encounters with some percipients. As I stated, John Keel and others have mentioned strange knockings and other poltergeist-type activity in association with UFO sightings or even the presence of these objects in a neighbourhood.

Given that this event happened one year, almost to the

minute, after the witness' UFO encounter, I feel inclined to place this account more in the category of a screen memory/UFO incident. This may, however, simply be my intuitive feeling. This story does not have the intuitive "feel" of a Black Dog encounter.

No colour is ascribed to the dog in the second story, nor are we given any other markers for our apparition such as the glowing red eyes. We are only told that it was quite large and that, after the sighting of the dog, a UFO encounter occurred immediately thereafter. We know that high strangeness often produces panic reactions in ordinary canines so this could simply have been a large dog frightened by the incoming UFO and trying to vacate the area.

While the account is certainly strange, and strangeness is sometimes known to happen in clusters, there does not seem to be definitive reason to believe that this was a sighting of a Phantom Black Dog. As an unidentified craft is also front and center in this incident, the screen-memory theory must also be considered.

The Black Dog's association with storms, its ability to talk and its appearance along with unidentified craft in the sky are not well-proven attributes of the phantom in its lore. Given some of the incidents that we will see in the chapter titled Random Oddities later in the book, I will not say that these things are impossible, just that they have not been borne out by the lore ... so far.

In the next section, the idea that this apparition is cognizant of and pays attention to its witnesses is explored. The lore evidence for this behaviour is much more extensive.

13

THE BLACK DOG STARE

ONE OF THE truly interesting aspects of the Black Dog subject is that, unlike spectral apparitions that seem to be psychic recordings of an event and to completely ignore the observer, the Black Dog is stated, again and again, to be aware of the witness. This observation happens so frequently that the author has named it the Black Dog Stare.

In many witness accounts, the Dog will look intently at the witness, sometimes even turning its head to do so. In a later section on Black Dogs that seem to change size and even shape, you will hear the story of Ronda, whose encounter with a Black Dog near Amarillo, Texas, began with the animal staring intently at her before the real strangeness commenced.

Janet and Colin Bord, in their book *Alien Animals*, make quite a point of the Stare, saying:

> It often seems that the dog is definitely aware of the witness, and makes a point of looking at him ... In fact the dog not only looks at the witness, he stares at him, or turns his head so that he can look at him. This acts as a strong link between the two, and may mean that the dog's appearance in front of a

particular witness is intentional and has some personal significance for the witness.

The Bords might have a point here. As I've mentioned and as we will explore in depth shortly, many times the Black Dog appears to a person either as an omen of impending death or as a guardian. In both instances, the Dog would seem to be quite intentional about its appearance, and the apparition definitely has personal significance to the percipient. This significance may not be evident in all of the Black Dog stories, but, like the death motif, its appearance seems to be observed well above the level of chance.

The Bords highlight this aspect of the Black Dog phenomenon with some short vignettes.

In 1927, on the Isle of Man, a friend of the Manx author Walter Gill encountered a Black Dog near Ramsey. The beast was shaggy-coated and had the usual eyes like "coals of a fire" and as often happens with the Black Dog, the creature would not let Gill's friend pass. The two stood looking at each other until the Dog finally moved so that the witness could get by. In a postscript to this adventure, the witness' father died shortly thereafter.

A Cornish witness named Samuel Drew stated that the Black Dog he encountered "went close by me, and as it passed, it turned upon me and my companions huge fiery eyes that struck terror to all our hearts".

A Cambridgeshire witness stated that the Dog he witnessed glared at him like "an old bull". Those who have been on the receiving end of a bull's stare will know that the glare from a bull is a signal that one should exit the area, quickly.

In Ireland, a female witness near Ballaghaderreen in County Roscommon described seeing a Black Dog that turned its head to look at her and how its eyes were "almost human in their intelligence".

The final notation on this subject in the Bord book tells of a schoolmaster living in Ballygar, County Galway, Ireland, who had a classic Black Dog encounter, with the Dog following him as he cycled along a country lane. This gentleman stated that the Dog looked up at him "in a way that made me feel uneasy" although the schoolmaster was not certain why he felt that way.

There are other accounts of the Black Dog Stare on the *Shuckland* website. Witness Arthur Durose recounts a story from his time of service in World War II:

In the early years of World War Two I was stationed on an airfield at Oulton in Norfolk. Sometime in the Winter of '41-42 I was walking alone from Aylsham to Oulton Street. The night was very cold but clear. I had just passed [on the B1354] Blickling Hall on my right when to my surprise I suddenly saw a large black dog standing in the middle of the road some few feet from me ... As I called to the dog a most peculiar feeling came upon me. The nearest description I can give is that it was a "nervous tingling". I advanced towards the animal but as I went forward the animal retreated but without moving its feet, almost as though it was a cardboard "cut-out" being pulled away from me with strings.

The dog's mouth was open but it made no sound. The animal was not in a belligerent attitude but just seemed to be observing me. I stopped and the dog also ceased its backward motion. After regarding me for maybe ten seconds the animal just completely disappeared. By "disappeared" I mean that it did not run away but literally "disappeared". The night was very clear and I had a good view over the paddocks to my left and right. I could see no dog.

Mr. Durose goes on to assure those reading the account, as many witnesses do, that he had consumed no alcohol that night.

As a side note, I find the assertion of drunkenness as a cause for an incident of high strangeness to be silly in the extreme. Alcohol consumption, by itself, does not cause hallucinations. There are rare cases of alcohol-induced hallucination, but these only seem to occur in instances of extreme alcohol abuse. Alcohol might dull the senses and make one less observant, but it certainly does not cause the vast majority of users to hallucinate.

The Durose account is interesting not only for the Dog's intense regard, but also for the odd detail of the animal moving away from him without seeming to move its legs. This oddity seems to take this sighting firmly into the realm of high strangeness. Interestingly, Blickling Hall has another Black Dog sighting associated with it that we will encounter later.

Before departing this topic, *Shuckland* also gives us two stories from the vicinity of the Coltishall Bridge in Norfolk.

In the early 1950s, a young lady and her beau were passing time on the aforementioned bridge at dusk when they noted a Black Dog that the woman first mistook for a pony (another instance of the extreme size of this apparition). The animal was approaching from a crossroads and, as it walked by them, turned its head to look at them.

The Dog vanished before it finished crossing the bridge, and both witnesses experienced the frequently noted fear reaction. The witness was reported to still have hesitation about using the bridge years later, further evidence of the impression that such encounters make on the percipients.

The second incident occurred on Coltishall High Street just after exiting the bridge. Late at night, two Royal Air Force officers were returning to their base in a Mini automobile. Just as they turned onto High Street from the Coltishall Bridge, they were forced to brake hard as an "enormous black dog" crossed the road.

The creature resembled a Labrador retriever, but its back was level with the roof of the vehicle. The witnesses stated that the roof was 1.35 metres tall, so that would equal about 53 inches. To give some context here, the tallest dog on record was a Great Dane that measured 44 inches at the shoulder. Thus, this animal would have been approximately nine inches taller than the tallest dog in *The Guinness Book of World Records*! The officers further stated:

> As it loped across our line of sight it slowly turned its head, to glare directly and disdainfully into our astonished faces, presenting us with a pair of fiery red eyes. It then slowly swung back its head and continued its measured progress onto the cobbles ... that stretched up to the shops/houses on the far side of the road. As it hit the cobbles, it quite literally vanished ...

This account makes one wonder why the Dog was so "disdainful" of these two and how the two came to that conclusion about the creature's regard. Perhaps it did not approve of whatever the two officers had been up to that evening and decided to give them a cosmic wake-up call? Or maybe the Dog simply didn't think the two were worthy of its attention and went about its business.

Whatever the cause, the Phantom Black Dog, unlike many apparitions, often seems to be aware of the witness and goes to great pains to make its regard evident.

Perhaps the most famous, or infamous, of the Phantom Black Dog's associations is its reputation as a foreteller of death. In the next chapter, we will explore that relationship in depth.

14

OMEN OF DEATH

FOR THOSE WHO have a passing familiarity with the Phantom Black Dog mythos, one of the first things that comes to mind about the Dog is that it is supposed to be a harbinger of death. While it will be shown that this aspect is but a part of the Black Dog folklore, it is a large part and definitely deserves to be discussed.

As I currently reside in Canada, it seems fitting that discussion of the Black Dog as a death harbinger begin with a very strange story from Nova Scotia. This tale comes to us courtesy of M. L. Fraser in the book *Folklore of Nova Scotia*.

The story is set in Antigonish Harbour, Nova Scotia, where we meet a man who is a "confirmed drunkard" who accompanies young Dan M (the name is abbreviated in the text to preserve the witness' identity) down to the town of Antigonish. The two men part in the village with the agreement that they will meet up in the afternoon to head home.

As such stories go, events did not work out as agreed. The two men were very late arriving home, and fearing that they had been spooked off their horses by the "things" on North River hill, Dan's mother sent out a rescue party in the form of Dan's younger brother, Alex.

Alex followed the same "bridge path" that the two men should have taken, and found Dan having "a dreadful time to keep his companion on his horse".

The two brothers did not want to return the drunkard to his widowed mother, so they decided to take him back to Alex's home. Before they reached the house, though, they noticed a "big black dog" following them. Attempts to drive the animal away were unsuccessful.

The two intrepid M brothers got their burden back to the house and, locking the door against the dog, hauled him up the back stairs and into bed, trying to avoid Alex's father, who opposed alcohol.

To their horror, when the two men come back downstairs, the Black Dog had "passed through the closed door". The Dog proceeded up the stairs after his apparent victim but for some reason was unable to pass the bedroom of Alex's two young sisters at the head of the stairs.

The dog travelled up and down the stairs all night, and Alex knelt at the drunken man's bedside, praying fervently that the inebriate might be spared since death, in the form of the Black Dog, appeared to be imminent. Apparently, Alex had a direct line to his deity since the dog had disappeared by the morning, and the drunkard woke sober (and, one would expect, quite hungover).

In an interesting follow-up to the story, the brothers M told the story to their horse-challenged acquaintance, and the fellow was "so much affected that he reformed completely and died a good death at home years later". The writer attests that they had the story from the niece of Alex, who told the girl the story himself.

I am interested in why the Black Dog could not pass the

bedroom of the younger sisters. This particular Dog did not seem to be bound to a specific territory, nor was it stopped by a mere door. What was it about passing that bedroom that stopped this apparition in its tracks and sent it travelling up and down the stairs all night?

Now, in this story, the Dog does not presage the man's death, but it is evident that the local people knew of this apparition and its reputation for predicting death, and they did all that they could to protect the drunkard.

Canada is not the only place where the Black Dog is associated with death. In *Haunted Places in the South*, Alan Brown gives the following brief account from the southern United States:

> A few months later, the mysterious black dog made another appearance. A man named Williams and his family were coming home from church when the great black dog ran out of the woods. When it reached the William's [sic] wagon, it stopped, looked at Mr. Williams, barked and disappeared. Two weeks later, Mr. Williams died.

Now, this one case could be a coincidence but when one moves on to Connecticut, one encounters an interesting variation of our apparition called the Black Dog of the Hanging Hills. In an article in the Connecticut Weekender, Sean Henri tells his readers to "Go Searching for the Legendary Black Dog of the Hanging Hills". After reading the article, one might wonder why one would do such a thing.

Henri begins by quoting a witness who is repeating an oft-told phrase about this Dog: "If you meet the Black Dog once, it shall be for joy; if twice, it shall be for sorrow; and the third time shall bring death". The author then goes on to tell us the story of W. H. C. Pynchon, the individual who made that statement, and Pynchon's friend Herbert Marshall of the US Geological Survey.

Pynchon, also a geologist, and Marshall were studying rocks near a reservoir in the area and saw a little dog running toward them, "excitedly wagging its tail". Both knew the legend of the small black dog that appeared, making no sounds and leaving no footprints, and both had seen the dog before. Though he scoffed at the local tales, this was Marshall's third time being in the presence of the silent creature.

As the dog drew closer, Marshall slipped on ice and fell to his death. This was Pynchon's second sighting of the dog, and he met with the great sadness of losing his friend almost immediately. One wonders if Mr. Pynchon avoided that area like the plague after this run-in with a pint-sized Black Dog.

The place where this Black Dog is sighted is Hubbard Park in Meriden, Connecticut, but if the reader chooses to check it out, it is strongly recommended that, should you see a small black dog, you not return for a second look! In the local lore, the first viewing of the Black Dog is harmless and might even be for the good. Subsequent viewings, however, reportedly result in sadness and then death.

It is also worth noting that, as I have mentioned previously, Meriden, Connecticut, and Meridean, Wisconsin, both have Black Dog lore attached to them.

Adam Zmarzlinski gives us another American Black Dog story in his article "The Black Dog: Origins and Symbolic Characteristics of the Spectral Canine". Zmarzlinski relates a story from the 1943 winter issue of *Hosier Folklore Bulletin* in which a local journalist tells the tale of Johnnie who travelled across the Irish section of Detroit, Michigan, dubbed Corktown, to visit a friend with his mother:

We'd not gone far ... before Mother said, "Something's wrong, Johnnie," and a few steps after that, we saw a black dog running in front of us. He was a great big son of a gun, and all black as tar. First, he'd run before us and then behind us, but he never left us alone for a minute. "We're turning back," says Mother, "for when my father died, a black dog ran along the roof and howled the whole night."

Johnnie goes on to say that the next day his mother's friend was murdered. If it were not for Johnnie's own testimony that he saw the Dog, one might conjecture that Johnnie's mother had that mixed blessing and curse the Irish call the Second Sight or just the Sight. Spontaneous psychic occurrences and the possibility of transmitting those occurrences will be examined later in the book.

As a final American tale, an unlikely source for accounts of the Black Dog arises: truck drivers. Annie Wilder, in her book *Trucker Ghost Stories: And Other True Tales of Haunted Highways*, gives the story of Jeff T. As with many truckers, Jeff drove long hours and says honestly that he has been so tired that he "blanked out for a few seconds" and that this had happened "more times than [he] can remember".

This driver fatigue is important to Jeff's account of driving on I-81 in Tennessee late on a clear night. Suddenly, a large shape crosses in front of his truck from left to right at "a rapid speed". Jeff states that the creature "looked like a large dog" and had "silvery-black hair – bushy hair". The encounter happened so quickly that Jeff did not glean many details of his Dog before it disappeared below his hood.

The trucker thought he had hit the dog, but when the mechanics checked his truck over, there was no sign the man had been in a collision. He forgot about the Black Dog until he sat talking with another driver who stated, matter-of-factly, that there was a "black dog that drivers who are really tired sometimes see at night. He told me that it was a harbinger of death, meaning: 'Park now and sleep, or die in the wreck waiting for you just up the road'".

Truckers spend a lot of time on the road. Given the Black Dog's love for roadsides, it seems almost implausible that we wouldn't have at least one Black Dog tale from a trucker. Personally, I find this tale intriguing due to the matter-of-fact nature of the other trucker's statements about the Black Dog and his seeming nonchalance about conveying this information. If driving fatigued is as common as Jeff T seems to indicate, I plan to give trucks an even wider berth on the road.

As has been noted earlier in the text, the truly in-depth research on the Phantom Black Dog comes out of the United Kingdom. Consideration of the Black Dog as a death apparition in this context yields a vein so rich that one could likely fill a small book with stories devoted to this single topic. This text will present a cross-section of stories from folklorists and others.

First of all, please note that the researcher Ivan Bunn in an article on Black Shuck, one of the Black Dog's many names, notes that "the facts do not compare favourably to the legends [of Shuck being a foreteller of death], for out of 74 stories so far collected, only 17 instances of death followed when the witness actually attributed the death to the encounter ..."

This supposition seems rather inaccurate since, looking at Bunn's own figures, we can say that over 20% of his witnesses experienced a death in the family after their sighting. I'm not a statistician, but it seems to me that this would be statistically significant and, therefore, a notable attribute of the Black Dog.

In that same article, Bunn tells of a letter that he received in 1977 relating an encounter that happened near Buxton Lamas Church, Norfolk, in 1930. The witness stated that a "large, black shaggy dog" appeared at his side from nowhere, and when the witness tried to pat the "old fellow", the dog promptly disappeared. The witness received a letter that his brother had died in

"Liverpool Hospital the previous Friday ... at the exact same time I [the witness] encountered the dog ..."

This incident with its church, vanishing dog and death portent is a classic Black Dog tale, but it is one of many in the haunted isles of Britain. The witness' attempt to pat the Black Dog is notable. Not all of these apparitions appear in the terrifying, glowing-eyed form. As we've seen, witnesses sometimes mistake the Black Dog for an ordinary dog until the apparition disappears or turns glowing eyes on them.

Katharine Briggs, one of Britain's foremost folklorists, tells a story of the Skriker, another Black Dog name, in her book *A Dictionary of British Folk-Tales in the English Language*. In her characteristic, storytelling style, Briggs opens the story thus:

> One winter's night a young man named Adam left the Patten Arms at Chipping to return to his cottage, three or four miles away on the banks of the Hodder. In the light of the moon Parlick, Longridge, Thornley height, and Kemple End could be seen, and far up the valley lay the fells beyond Whitewell.
>
> About midnight a cloud covered the moon, the wind began to rise, and the noise of the rising storm seemed to Adam to bring with it such fiendish cries and shrieks, that his courage almost failed, and he longed to turn back. But he had already come far, and knew that if he could cross the bridge ahead of him, he would be out of reach of the spirits of that place, who were not able to cross the water ...

Poor Adam, struggling against this storm, has even worse luck as he tries to cross the aforementioned bridge. There in the midst of his path home stands the Skriker, "covered with shaggy black hide, and its huge eyes blaz[ing] like fire ..." The Skriker began to trail Adam, stopping and moving as the man did, until Adam's nerve broke and he ran.

The Black Dog chased Adam until he tripped over a stone, and then disappeared. The man struggled on, hearing shrieking that we must presume came from the creature and then encountered the Skriker again on the next bridge that he came to. As before, the apparition paced the man until he arrived back at his cottage. When his wife answered his frantic knocks on the door, Adam "[falls] to the ground in a dead swoon" from which it takes the frightened wife some time to bring him back to consciousness.

Within the space of a few days, Adam's eldest child drowned, and his wife died of a fever. Adam himself went mad and spent the rest of his days looking for "imaginary spectres".

This account is terribly sad, but the thing that stands out to me is that Adam thought he would be safe once he crossed the first bridge, that is passed over running water, but, instead, the Skriker chased him until he fell, disappeared and then picked up the chase on another bridge.

Obviously, the Phantom Black Dog does not have the aversion to running water that other spirits in folklore display unless that running water happens to be the boundary of its seeming territory. We see this happen in the story of the Demon Dog of Valle Crucis.

Mark Norman, in his extensive book *Black Dog Folklore*, relates a story from a letter that he received in 1958. This tale came from the Haynes family, which Norman states was rumoured to be haunted by a Black Dog. Family hauntings by Black Dogs are encountered in the legends, but this is the only instance I found in a witness statement.

In any case, the writer speaks of a time when she was on a driving tour with their mother along the West Coast of England and Scotland. The letter writer states that a Black Dog began following their vehicle at Durham and that, oddly, when they stopped to feed the horses, the mother ordered food to be left out for the animal.

Undeterred, as the two proceeded with their tour, the dog appeared at "the usual hundred yards ahead of us and was still with us till we got over the Border". The witness' mother took ill at Skelmorlie, a village in North Ayrshire, Scotland, on the River Clyde, and was "taken home to Liverpool where she died ..." The writer notes that they "always said the Black Dog was a haunt".

It's interesting to note, in this account, that the Black Dog appears in broad daylight and appears to lead whatever conveyance the witness was travelling in. Both of these items are uncharacteristic of our apparition, which tends to prefer the dusk hours and the hours of the night for its appearances and is well known for pacing beside travellers, not leading them by a hundred yards.

The other idiosyncrasy in this story is the business of leaving food for the animal. People with animist beliefs often leave offerings for spirits, so I have to wonder if the mother in this story was trying to buy off this spirit, perhaps because she understood what its presence meant.

From a personal letter to the *Shuckland* website, we learn the following about a witness who went for a night hike with a group of Venture Scouts and Ranger Guides in the area of Great Massingham, Norfolk. This presumed scout was a short distance past a point called Shepherd's Bush when he saw what he thought was a sheep dog bounding toward him.

At a range of twenty yards, the creature supposedly leapt at the witness, causing him to drop to his knees and try to shield himself from what he perceived as an attack. When there was no contact, the witness stood up quickly, sure that he was going to be hit from behind, but found himself alone.

The witness described his "attacker" as "a big black dog in

the order of a very large St. Bernard with a wide mouth, teeth very evident, and two largish eyes amongst a mass of black fur".

The witness noted that he had never heard local Black Dog lore until this event, and though he assigned it to pure chance, precisely one year later the witness was involved in a "road traffic accident as a pedestrian". This young person was left in hospital for three and a half months but fortunately survived.

The witness makes light of the death omen part of the Black Dog legend by saying, "well the old bugger had a darned good try!" It should be remembered that the Dog is also said to be a portent of disaster in this part of the UK, so perhaps our witness should not be so blasé.

I would also note a feature in the description that we see cropping up in some Black Dog cases. The witness says that the teeth of this animal were very evident along with the requisite eyes. We will see this description again, along with witnesses who describe the Dog's mouth or tongue as bright red. This might simply be a result of the witness' fear of being bitten, something like looking down the barrel of a gun that is pointed at you, but it is worth noting.

For our final death omen story, we turn to prolific Fortean author Nick Redfern. In an article for *The Unexplained Mysteries* website, Redfern tells the 1972 story of Nigel Lea, which took place in the Cannock Chase region of the UK. Redfern has a particular obsession with the high strangeness in the Chase, and after reviewing this story, one can see why.

Mr. Lea's incident began with something unusual in a Black Dog story, a light anomaly. The witness was driving and saw "glowing blue light" strike the ground and explode into a "torrent of bright, fiery sparks". As he drove up to the spot where he thought the light had impacted, he spotted another anomaly: "the biggest bloody dog [he] had ever seen in [his] life".

The beast was described as "muscular and black, with large,

pointed ears and huge paws". In addition, Mr. Lea states that the Dog carried a great deal of negative energy with it and that it "had a wild, staring look in its yellow-tinged eyes". The two looked at each other for a short period of time, and then the Black Dog backed slowly away into the forest.

Two or three weeks later, one of Mr. Lea's close friends was killed in a terrible industrial accident.

As can be clearly seen, from stories coming from both sides of the proverbial pond, the Phantom Black Dog is often cast as a foreteller of death. Furthermore, given Ivan Bunn's notations about the frequency with which someone in a witness' family or the witness themselves dies after sighting a Black Dog, and given the prevalence with which this death foretelling appears in the lore, it seems that the Phantom Black Dog truly does bear the role of death portent.

While this grim fact sits at the forefront of the reader's consciousness, another, even darker aspect of the Black Dog phenomenon must be discussed. There are recorded instances of the Black Dog not just foretelling death but actually causing it. These frightening tales are next in the survey.

15

BRINGER OF DEATH

ABRAHAM FLEMING PUBLISHED a strange little tract in 1577 the title
of which begins, *A Strange and Terrible Wonder* (title transliter-
ated into Modern English for clarity's sake). Fleming is obviously a preacher or religionist of some sort, for he frames his
story in terms of a warning from his god for errant sinners to
turn from their evil ways and back to whatever brand of Christianity he espoused. Nevertheless, the story that he tells is one of
the classics of Black Dog lore and is oft repeated.

According to Fleming, the action occurs on 4 August 1577
amidst "a great tempest of violent rain, lightning, and thunder,
the like whereof was seldom seen". Despite the terrible storm or,
perhaps because of it, the people of the parish of Bungay gath-
ered to "hear divine service and common prayer". According to
Fleming, the rain, thunder and lightning were such that the
people were struck with a "sore and sudden fear, they were
robbed of their right wits".

As the people prayed, there suddenly appeared "a dog as
they might discern it, of a black colour: at the sight whereof
together with fearful flashes of fire" led the congregation to
assume that doomsday had come.

The Black Dog, which Fleming immediately takes for the Devil, runs to and fro in the church and then passes between two kneeling congregants and "wrung the necks of them both at one instant clean backward" such that "they strangely died".

One generally dies when one's neck is wrung backwards, but the question here is: what was the mechanism of injury? We could understand the victims being mauled by a large canid, but how did this Black Dog wring the necks of two men? Did the beast suddenly develop hands and the musculature to accomplish this task? Or was the wringing accomplished by psychokinesis or some strange, kinetic magical power?

The Black Dog wasn't finished with this congregation, however. The creature passed by another man and "gave him such a gripe on the back, that therewithal he was presently drawn together and shrunk up, as it were a piece of leather scorched in a hot fire".

Fleming notes that the man who was gripped lived, but one wonders what sort of life he had after this adventure. Being shrunk like a "piece of leather in a hot fire" does not seem conducive to normal function afterwards. Also, if this were a Black Dog on a rampage in the church, how was the creature able to grab someone? Again, the implication seems to be that whatever was loose in this church had hands with which to grip a person.

The archaic usage of the term gripe seems to indicate that the beast, whatever it was, grasped and then controlled this poor fellow. For context, the dictionary uses the example of a miser who gripes money. This whole business of wringing necks and gripping people brings to mind our earlier discussion of the Black Dog in relation to Beowulf's Grendel.

As proof of his testimony, Fleming notes that there are "in the stones of the Church, and likewise in the Church door which are marvellously rent & torn, the marks as it were of his claws or talons". The church doors at Bungay still bear a set of scorch marks of unknown provenance, said to be the claw marks of this rogue entity.

Curiously, Fleming also mentions that the Clark (from Old English *clerc, which refers to a learned man or clergyman)* of the church was cleaning the gutters when all this occurred and was "smitten down ... with a violent clap of thunder" (struck by lightning?). Amazingly, this fellow is said to have taken no harm in the incident, but "the wires, wheels, and other things belonging to the Clark were wrong asunder, and broken in pieces". Fleming cites this damage as further proof of the Dog's physical presence although the reason why is not clear.

One wonders how it is that the "clark" of the church was cleaning gutters in a storm of this magnitude and how the people of the church were hearing "divine service and common prayer" if the "clark" was up in the gutters.

Fleming's account moves on without addressing any of these discontinuities. On the same day, in the town of Blythburgh, a similar beast appeared in that town's church and, after some acrobatics amongst the ceiling beams, "slew two men and a lad, and burned the hand of another person ...". Fleming relates that the fiend then "flew with wonderful force to no little fear of the assembly, out of the Church in a hideous and hellish likeness".

After telling us this horrific tale, the author then presents a prayer of repentance and protection and closes his tract.

Although this tract is one of the most often referenced pieces of literature regarding the Black Dog, this encounter is legendary and is certainly not citing witnesses to the event. Fleming was a translator and editor for several London printing houses, and it is likely that the tract was the result of exaggerated oral accounts. Notably, in Bungay itself, the scorch marks on the church door are called the Devil's Fingerprint, and other local accounts of the event attribute it to the Devil himself, not a Black Dog.

While I feel certain that the peasants of Bungay and Blythburgh encountered something they could not explain that day in 1577, given the discontinuities in the story itself and the contradictory folklore, I don't think we can use this legendary account, which is not supported by any witness statements, as evidence of the Black Dog's murderous intent.

As I mentioned earlier, the Fleming tract is one of the classics of Black Dog lore, but it is not the only example of a Black Dog supposedly doing a human harm. In some cases, it was believed that the delayed shock of seeing a Black Dog would kill a person. Katharine Briggs, in her book of British folk tales, gives us a story that was given to her by the mother of one of her friends.

The woman had lost a brother under very strange circumstances. The boy had been sent on an errand as the sun was going down. The lad got to his destination but found the house he had been sent to closed up, so he turned to leave. "A large black dog rose up silently from the ground and put his paws on the child's shoulders". The woman's brother had not seen the dog in the darkness, and, as you might imagine, it gave him quite a scare but, according to the narrative, "he recovered himself quickly and went home".

The lad mentioned the incident to his parents but didn't think much of it, as he had some studying to do for upcoming exams. The brother went to bed at his usual time, but, according to Briggs, the young man died in the middle of the night "from the delayed effects of shock".

As almost always occurs with Briggs' stories, the postscript is that the people the boy had been sent to visit had no dog at all, and the locals quickly ascribed the incident to the "barguest", one of the many names that the Black Dog answers to.

We have seen in the previous chapter that the Black Dog is certainly a foreteller of death. I see no reason to ascribe this boy's death to the phantom that he encountered. Rather, it seems to me that the Dog was simply performing its function of predicting the death of the lad.

I lay no claim to being a psychologist, but common sense tells us that parents have trouble accepting the death of a child. It seems likely to me that the Black Dog in this story acted as a scapegoat for the parents' grief at the boy's untimely demise.

Another story in which the Black Dog is blamed for death is also somewhat debatable, although this one seems to draw closer to the Black Dog being the cause rather than the foreteller of the death.

The reporter Stacia Briggs, writing in the *Eastern Daily Press*, quotes folklorist Ivan Bunn:

> The story is told of how at Rockland, Norfolk, one night, a man and his companion were driving along a lane "... when suddenly right in their path stood a huge uncanny dog. The driver pushed on in spite of his companion's warning ... but as the cart touched the Thing the air was alive with flames and a hideous, sulphurous stench loaded the atmosphere. Within a short time the overbold driver died and Shuck has not been seen since in these parts..."

This reporter, who does not seem to be related to Katharine Briggs, whom we have visited with previously, comments that the smell of "sulphur is often recorded by those who witness paranormal activities, and the smell has been recorded since biblical times and by the Greek philosophers – it is also remarked on by those who claim to have been visited by flying saucers or aliens ..." This is assuredly true and, for a deeper look at scents and the paranormal, one would do well to read Joshua Cutchin's book *The Brimstone Deceit*.

The question that faces the reader, however, is the question of causation. Again, someone who has contact with a Black Dog dies shortly thereafter. Is the creature's admittedly paranormal reaction – the flames and the stench – designed to cause death? If this were true, then how do we account for the many witnesses who have encountered similar phenomena in high strangeness encounters and lived to tell the tale?

There is also the matter of the survival of the other fellow in the cart. If the flames and smell had been intended to kill, then why did the second man survive?

Some writers assume that the Black Dog in this case was taking revenge for the cart driver's impertinence in moving forward when the Dog was obviously trying to halt his progress. I doubt that this was the case since this text contains many stories where people have tried to move a Black Dog or get rid of it, up to shooting at the entity, with no negative result or reaction from the stolid Dog.

While this account is remarkable for the fire and stench, it still seems to me that the Black Dog's presence could be explained as a death portent. Some people, perhaps, require a more blatant warning than others?

In the next chapter, we will see examples of Black Dogs blocking roads to prevent travel that would be hazardous to the percipient. I don't quite see how this function would fit with the details of the case, but it is something to bear in mind.

Regardless, this story is still ambiguous. The Black Dog might have been the proximate cause of the man's death, or it might not have been.

In *East Anglian Folklore and Other Tales*, W. H. Barrett remarks that a witness called C. Marlowe told him:

... an old salt asked me if I had ever heard of the "shuck Dog". It appeared that a spectre of this name was supposed to haunt the marshes between Wells and Sheringham (Norfolk) ... his grandfather apparently met the ghost near Stiffkey and had been found in the morning with his throat torn ... All the way from Weybourne Hoop the story was the same. A hound, much bigger than any animal of its kind, haunted the salt lands and pursued wayfarers ... leaping upon his victims from behind (he would maul the victim's throat and then vanish in smoke ...

Here, at last, we have a clear intimation that the Black Dog is actually responsible for the deaths of people, falling on them and tearing at their throats.

Our friend Stacia Briggs, writing in the *Eastern Daily Press*, notes that "the tales of Black Shuck were spread joyfully by smugglers who realised that the fear of a devil dog who could condemn you to death with a stare would keep people off coastal lanes at night while they got up to no good ..." Is it not possible that said smugglers did more than spread the tales? Perhaps, some particularly heinous criminals set a vicious dog or dogs loose and created the foundation for these tales.

Once again, it seems that we have to have some doubts about the Phantom Black Dog being the cause of death in Barrett's account. I am minded of A. Conan Doyle's classic *Hound of the Baskervilles* in which a dastardly individual murders a man with a weak heart using an enormous and very real dog painted up with phosphorescent paint. Imagine the effect of such an action on a populace already primed with legends of the ghostly Black Shuck. Any mauling would be laid at the spectre's feet without a thought.

Given what we already know and will see of the Black Dog, which seems to spend most of its time as a non-solid apparition, it seems unlikely to me that it would decide to assume solid form for the express purpose of murdering travellers in one specific area. Such behaviour seems very out of character for our phantom.

Our final entry in the contest for a killer Black Dog is the titular beast in the story of the Barguest of Troller's Gin, told to us by the inestimable Katharine Briggs:

> A young man of the neighbourhood once resolved to see this monster for himself, and set out on a windy, moonlight night to make his way to the Gill. It was too steep for the moonbeams to penetrate, and in the darkness, amid the sound of the raging water, he suddenly heard a loud cry, "Forbear!" He pressed on, however, and came to a great yew-tree, under which he drew on the ground a circle, uttering certain charms, bent down and kissed the ground three times, and called on the Spectre Hound to appear.
>
> A whirlwind sprang up, fire flashed from every cleft in the rocks, and with a wild bark, the hound sprang into view. In the morning, passing shepherds found the young man's dead body under the yew, with strange marks on his breast which seemed as though no human agency could have placed them there ...

A lot of people would look at this tale and think it was sheer poppycock, and it may well be. However, it should be remembered that there is a long history of magicians calling up entities of various sorts and also a long history of those summonings going wrong, in one way or the other.

I don't think we need to posit magic gone wrong in this tale though.

My primary issue with the story is point of view. It is possible that someone would know that this young man wanted to summon the Black Dog, and they might even know that he had "made his way to the Gill", but, unless they were with the hapless magician, how would they know the other details of the story?

While the point-of-view issue seems to drop this story into the category of legend, we also have the matter of the circle-casting under a yew tree as an indicator that the story is more symbolic and, perhaps, cautionary than actual fact. A yew tree, in British folklore and in the Celtic tree alphabet called Ogham, a form of divination, is symbolic of death and seems, in this account, to be a foreshadowing element of the young man's coming demise.

Finally, while we are told that the Black Dog does appear, there is no direct link between the Dog and the death of this lad in the story. The Dog appeared, and then the boy was found dead. We have no idea what happened to the would-be magician other than that he had "strange marks on his breast" and he was dead.

I am inclined to drop this bit of lore into the legend category given the point-of-view issue, the foreshadowing elements, and the unclear relationship between the young man's death and the supposedly successful evocation of a Black Dog.

Looking at the body of evidence for the Phantom Black Dog as a dangerous killer, I remain completely unconvinced. Bungay is a legend that comes down to us from a religionist determined to stir repentance in the hearts of his readers and using a devil in dog form to accomplish this.

Other stories have unclear causes of death and could as easily be portent-of-death stories as cause of death. The account of the Shuck Dogs of Norfolk seems certainly contrived by smugglers using tales or perhaps even real dogs to run people off the lonely coastal roads at night.

Even if we take the tale of the Barguest of Troller's Gin at face value, we cannot lay the death of the young man firmly at the Black Dog's feet since there seems to be no actual witness to the events. The "strange marks on his breast" are as likely to be the result of wildlife depredation as the claws, teeth or magic of an apparition.

As such, while it is clear that the Black Dog's story is intimately tied up with death, it is not clear that the phantom actually causes deaths. We will move on now to another major theme in the Black Dog lore – the idea that these apparitions actually appear to protect people in times of need.

16

GUARDIAN OF THE ROADS

I HAVE NOTED in my research that sightings of the Black Dog in the US tend more toward the death portent / scary Black Dog that Theo Brown would call a Type A apparition. I suspect that the reason for this is simply that Americans are not as familiar with tales of the Black Dog and, therefore, when they do encounter this apparition, view it with fear. As they do not have recourse to the copious folklore of the Black Dog, they are not familiar with the tales that follow. If they did, I suspect that more Americans might suspend judgement of the apparition when it appears on this side of the Atlantic.

I will begin this chapter with a pithy Canadian story. Katharine Briggs in her dictionary of British folk tales spoke with a witness who was eighty-five at the time of giving her narrative. This elderly woman had moved from Somerset in the UK to Canada and then back to the UK in her lifetime and tells us:

> When I was a young girl I was living outside Toronto in Canada and I had to go to a farm some miles away one evening. There were woods on the way and I was greatly afraid, but a

large black dog came with me and saw me safely to the door. When I had to return he again appeared, and walked with me till I was nearly home. Then he vanished.

One could be pardoned for looking at this account and thinking that the young girl had simply had the good fortune to attract the attention of a large, friendly canine, and perhaps this was the case, but we do note the classic indicator of a paranormal event in this account. The Black Dog vanishes at the end of its "mission".

This tale is only the first of such stories, and as with the death omen stories, we will see a clear pattern developing as we add more weight to the scales.

We find a treasure trove of guardian stories as we move to the UK.

Ethel Rudkin, a folklorist who lived in the Lincolnshire area of England, is perhaps the Black Dog's biggest proponent. She maintains, in her seminal article entitled simply "The Black Dog", that these creatures are, by and large, harmless and, indeed, quite helpful. Interestingly, the Dog seems to appear, in Lincolnshire at least, when it is most needed.

One witness told Ms. Rudkin of a time "when Crosby and Scunthorpe were both villages" that a certain woman had to make the journey from one of these villages to the other to do some shopping. As this woman was headed back to her home, she noticed a strange Black Dog walking behind her.

There is no record of the witness either encouraging the Dog or trying to shoo it away, but before long, she passed "some Irish labourers, and she heard them say what they would do to the lone woman if 'that (something) dog hadn't been with her'". The witness made it home without incident, but when she called to her spouse to come see her saviour, the Dog had vanished completely.

What is immediately noticeable in this story and those that follow is that the Black Dog, though huge, takes on a much more normal appearance for this guardian role. It is almost as if the phantom is trying not to scare the recipient of its protection. I often wonder though, if these men had been foolhardy enough to attack the lady, what they would have seen when the Black Dog came to her defence. Given other descriptions of the Dog, I suspect that glowing red eyes and huge teeth might have become more evident.

In another anecdote, Ms. Rudkin also tells the story of a lay Methodist preacher, whom we mentioned in the road-walking section, who was accompanied by a Black Dog during a walk in a dark wood and who believed that his companion had been sent to keep him safe during that walk. While there was no threat evident in that story there certainly was one in this tale from Norman's *Black Dog Folklore*. Coincidentally, this story, too, is about a Methodist preacher.

Norman states that the story appears in the April 1959 edition of the *Methodist Magazine* and that the article is by Ethel Whitaker. Ms. Whitaker states that her father, the Reverend Samuel Whitaker, was a circuit preacher in the Stroud district of Gloucestershire county in the early 1900s. The man of the cloth was returning from a pastoral care visit and had to walk some distance, late in the day. Apparently, Rev. Whitaker was not a large man, and just as he left the outskirts of a village, a "large black dog" appeared, walking by his side.

Again, there is no record of the reverend's reaction to the beast, but as the walk proceeded, the pastor was overtaken by two "large, brutal looking fellows" who stopped when they saw the dog, "scowled and passed on". As so often happens in these accounts, the Dog disappeared once the apparent threat had passed.

In an epilogue to the story, Ms. Whitaker states that her

father made inquiries in both villages, the people of whom he knew well, and no one recognized the dog he described. The good reverend never saw the creature again.

Again, the only hint that this Black Dog is anything other than a friendly canine is its habit of appearing when needed and then disappearing once the need has passed.

While we are on a slightly religious note, there is even a story of a Black Dog appearing as an apparent answer to prayer. Mark Norman tells of a witness who began their account, "My mother was not free from country superstitions, although she was a devoutly God fearing woman, with a firm faith in her God and a strong belief in the efficacy of prayer ..."

When this god-fearing woman was in her late teens, she needed to walk from Sampford Courtenay to Okehampton, West Devon, somewhere between five and six miles according to maps. In that time, the walk entailed passing through a section of dark woodland, and the lady was "very frightened for some reason that [the teller of the tale] cannot now remember, and in her fear prayed that she might have some companion to protect her".

It was not long before a large black dog "appeared in the wood and paced quietly by her side until she was entering the outskirts of Okehampton". Whether this answer to prayer came in the form of a physical dog or a Black Dog, we cannot really say, but the synchronicity of the animal appearing as the woman prayed is enough to be quite meaningful.

There is no note in the account about what happened with the Dog once the lady reached the outskirts of town. Perhaps, as with so many of these stories, it simply disappeared or walked into a hedge.

Now, there is no apparent threat in the above account, though one should never ignore an intuition of danger, but another yarn that comes to us from Mark Norman certainly has an air of foreboding. In this account, Norman relates the tale of a great personal friend of his family who, when she was in her teens, had to walk along a wood-lined road on her way to the village where she lived:

> One night in the gathering gloom, rather later than she could have wished, she was hurrying along when, to her alarm, she saw two disreputable tramps waiting just ahead. She hesitated, frightened and dismayed for a moment, when along in front of her there trotted a large black dog which she closely followed safely past the two men. They eyed her and the dog but did not dare to interfere. As she neared her home door, the dog was gone ...

Again, we see the Black Dog appearing when it is needed and then disappearing once the danger had passed.

From disreputable tramps to murder most foul, Katharine Briggs tells us yet another anecdote with a character named Johnnie, this one living in the UK, and as so often happens with these stories, the young man is walking home along a route that will take him through the woods:

> At the entrance of the wood a large black dog joined him, and pattered along by his side. He could not make out where it came from, but it never left him, and when the wood grew so dark that he could not see it, he still heard it pattering beside him. When he emerged from the wood, the dog had disappeared, and he could not tell where it had gone to. Well, Johnnie paid his visit, and set out to return the same way. At the entrance of the wood, the dog joined him, and pattered along beside him as before; but it never touched him, and he never spoke to it, and again, as he emerged from the wood, it ceased to be there.

This story, by itself, is eerie enough with the appearing and disappearing Dog, but it would not be remarkable in the annals of the Black Dog. The postscript to the tale certainly is:

> Years after, two condemned prisoners in York Gaol told the chaplain that they had intended to rob and murder Johnnie that night in the wood, but that he had a large dog with him, and when they saw that, they felt that Johnnie and the dog together would be too much for them.

Mark Norman has an issue with this story, which he also relates in his encyclopedic work. He asks how it is that the robbers' story, which seems to have been given under the seal of the confessional, became part of the public record. He also wonders how it is that the two miscreants, who had presumably lived a life of crime, remembered an incident in which they did not commit a crime, and that some years later.

I agree with Norman that this tale rests on the cusp of the legendary since there is no evident single witness. Nevertheless, I am moved to note that the criminals' memory might have been aided by the terror response noted in many Black Dog cases.

The Black Dog prevents a murder, in Johnnie's seemingly legendary story, and Briggs goes on to give us another interesting legend in which the Black Dog plays an integral part in bringing two murderers to justice.

A pair of robbers were well known for highway robbery along the Bath highway, but when they set a house afire to hide the robbery and the murder of a well-liked couple in the region, they had gone too far. A posse, such as one might have found in the Old West in the US, formed to bring the men to meet their Maker, and the outlaws led that band a merry chase.

As the pursuit progressed, the two were going to have to cross an area called the Down from Everley to Collingbourne

Kingston in Wiltshire County. There was a wood where they could take cover in that area, but the criminals had made a critical error. They had forgotten that the wood was the territory of a Black Dog!

The pair remembered this fact when they were confronted with "his huge gleaming eyes like saucers". The Dog was known to "bring ill to all who met him and death to the evil doer". Considering that the murder was not a day old, one might be forgiven for thinking these two were in for trouble.

The gleaming green eyes of the Dog appeared before them, and they "screamed and stumbled away along another path". That strategy availed them nothing, the gleaming eyes appeared again, and panicked, they ran from the forest and into the arms of their pursuers.

The posse men's only comment? "We knew we'd get them when they ran into the woods. All we had to do was wait outside, and the Black Dog [would] send 'em back".

Briggs, in her characteristic fashion, attaches a little postscript, noting that the murderers were hanged, but that the Black Dog was still seen into the twentieth century. As often happens with Briggs' stories, there seems to be an element of legend here since the story is told in the third person. How do we know what went on with the criminals in the woods? I include this tale since it is often cited in works on the Phantom Black Dog and, given all the legends about the apparition being a bearer of death and misfortune, in the interest of balanced coverage.

In a more modern account from Christopher Reeve's *A Straunge and Terrible Wunder*, witness E. Ramsey gives us another account of a Black Dog encountered while cycling. In this case, Mr. Ramsey was cycling home to Bawburgh, Norfolk, from playing darts in Norwich. He spotted the Black Dog with the characteristic eyes glowing like coals sitting next to a signpost, and sped up to get by the animal. He thought he was clear of the beast but then heard it coming up behind him, "his paws beating the grit road".

Ramsey feared he was about to be attacked from behind, but the Dog passed him, so close that he could smell its "rankness". Once the animal was ahead of him, it stopped near an area of small trees and bushes, called a spinney in Britain, and turned to face the witness, not looking at all friendly. The cyclist got off his bicycle, again fearing that he was about to be mauled, and keeping his conveyance between himself and the Dog.

During this stand-off, a vehicle came crashing out of the spinney, with no lights showing at all, "careering from side to side", and appeared to hit the Black Dog. Ramsey got clear of the wildly maneuvering car and ended up in a hedge with his cycle on top of him as the wayward vehicle roared away for parts unknown.

The witness got to his feet and was astounded to see that the Dog was still standing there even though the cyclist was sure it had been clobbered by the car. As the witness began to feel his fear returning, the Dog simply turned and vanished.

Although Ramsey had heard the legends of the Black Dog as a death omen, in this case, he was certain the beast had saved his life by delaying him. If the cyclist had been riding through the spot where the Black Dog was standing, he would have been hit by the speeding car and seriously injured or killed.

The Dog's behaviour in this account is strikingly blasé. It encounters the witness, gets ahead of him, stops him in the road and then seemingly gets hit by a car, only to shrug this off and walk off into the ether. It would be interesting to know what the driver of the wayward car did or did not see and if the incident provoked some change in habits for this careless individual, as was seen in the tale of the Antigonish Harbour drunkard in a previous section. Hopefully, the reckless driver had a moment of reckoning when he or she was faced with the enormous Black Dog in the road.

Another story of the Black Dog saving a life is also notable in that the witness actually had physical contact with the apparition. This tale comes to us from Katharine Briggs in her encyclopedic work on British folk tales:

> A more indisputably Somerset story was told [to] me by a very sweet and gentle cottager who had once had occasion to climb the Quantocks one winter afternoon. When he had climbed up Weacombe to the top the sea-mist came down, and he felt he might be frozen to death before he got home. But as he was groping along he suddenly touched shaggy fur and thought that old Shep, his sheep-dog, had come out to look [for] him. "Good dog, Shep. Whoame, boy!" he said. The dog turned and led him right to his cottage door, where he heard his own dog barking inside. He turned to look at the dog who had guided him, which grew gradually larger and then faded away. "It was the Black Dog, God bless it!" he would always say. It is unusual for anybody to touch the Black Dog without coming to harm.

Touching the Black Dog is very rare in the annals of the folklore; so rare, in fact, that I do not think Briggs can make the assertion that touching the Dog causes harm without supporting it further, which she does not.

Another, similar story involved James Murray, the first editor of the *Oxford English Dictionary*, and is told to us by Mark Norman. Murray actually had two encounters with the Black Dog, but this one was the most notable.

The incident took place in 1875 on a mountain that was not named in the story. Norman posits that "it is probable as it is around the same time that he was on a visit to Ambleside in the Lake District, the events take place somewhere in Cumbria ..."

The editor was on an outing in the mountains with his children when a dense fog rolled in. The group apparently tried to continue on, but a Black Dog "appeared" before them and would not let them proceed.

Eventually, the mist cleared, and Murray and his children found that the apparition had prevented them from blundering over a "dangerous precipice". The Dog had disappeared.

While there is no indication that the man or his children tried to touch this Black Dog, it is evident that the creature acted in a manner that made it clear they could not pass. Given this story and the story of the cyclist who was blocked from a disastrous accident by a Black Dog, one might begin to think that those instances of a Black Dog being aggressive might be instances of the apparition trying to redirect a person to a safer path.

Now, this panoply of tales should convince the reader that there is something more to the Phantom Black Dog than simply its talents as a seer of doom. Again and again, in the annals of Black Dog lore, just as one becomes convinced that all the legends of the Black Dog describe a creature of ominous habits, one comes across one of these stories, or a whole set of stories in which the Black Dog appears to protect the weak.

In reading the guardian accounts, I was struck by a repeated point. Most often, the Dog seems to appear to protect the innocent or, at least those who might be seen as innocent: a preacher walking home from doing his duty, a young girl returning home late at night through no fault of her own, a harmless person about to be set upon by ruffians, or a man and his children about to blunder over a cliff.

We cannot be certain, of course, but the Black Dog seems to have clear agency. It chooses whom it portends death to and whom it guards along the roads. As we saw in chapter 13, Colin and Janet Bord go so far as to state that "that the dog's appearance in front of a particular witness is intentional and has some personal significance for the witness." After reading many Black Dog stories, I am inclined to agree with the Bords.

Besides its propensity for foretelling death and guarding travellers, the Phantom Black Dog is well known for a number of other unusual traits. In the next chapter, we will look at the ability of our subject to seemingly appear and disappear at will and even to be invisible.

17

NOW YOU SEE IT …

ONE OF THE witness observations that sets the Phantom Black Dog apart from cryptid creatures is its observed propensity to vanish or be invisible to some observers. While several of the writers on this phenomenon agree that there are Black Dogs that have been handled or had physical effects in their environment such as rustling the leaves of a hedge or the sound of pattering feet, the vast majority of stories show a creature that seems ephemeral, at best.

In an excellent example of both insubstantiality and vanishing, Rudkin tells the story of Mrs. GB. This erstwhile lady was "in service" at Grayingham, Lincolnshire, and would go, of an evening, to meet with her young man. These dates seemed to be walking engagements, as the two would part at Blyborough, and GB would walk on home alone. On one such evening, GB became aware of a large Black Dog following her.

Apparently, GB was not the scaredy-cat sort. She slowed down to allow the animal to catch up to her and then attempted to wallop it with an umbrella to get it to leave her be. GB "nearly fainted" when the umbrella passed straight through its target, but the Dog seemed unfazed. It "trotted on beside her to the ash tree at the end of Chapels Lane where he vanished up the tree, or into the tree ..."

I did a little research on the older style of umbrella, and such an item, with its steel ribs, would have been a formidable weapon. It's also interesting that the Black Dog had no reaction to this aggression but simply continued on before disappearing into or up a tree, behaviour we have seen before.

Even more frightening is the story from Theo Brown of another woman who encountered a Black Dog in the aptly named Dog Lane, now called Haye Lane in Uplyme on the Devon-Dorset border. This Dog exhibits the traits of being invisible to all but the percipient and then vanishing to make things even more strange.

As I was returning to Lyme ... one night with my husband down Dog Lane, as we reached about the middle of it, I saw an animal about the size of a dog meeting us. "What's that?" I said to my husband. "What?" said he, "I see nothing." I was so frightened I could say no more then, for the animal was within two or three yards of us, and had become as large as a young calf, but had the appearance of a black shaggy dog with fiery eyes .... He passed close by me, and made the air cold and dank as he passed along. Though I was afraid to speak, I could not help turning round to look after him, and I saw him growing bigger and bigger as he went along, till he was as high as the trees by the roadside, and then seeming to swell into a large cloud, he vanished in the air.

The witnessed subject displays the remarkable ability to change size, a trait that will be discussed in a later chapter of the book. Note, too, that the passage of the Dog brought with it a classic sign of ghostly or paranormal presence, a cold spot.

Ghost hunters see cold spots as clear signs of spook

activity in their area, and some even theorize that these chilly spots are caused by entities drawing energy from the area so that they can manifest. This theory seems as likely as any given the presence of the large entity only feet away from the witness.

As we have noted, Black Dogs seem to love any long, straight stretch of travel as a gentleman in Cromer, Norfolk, noted to Ivan Bunn, the folklorist. This witness was "looking towards the railway bank" and saw a large black animal "sort of jumping and gliding quite fast towards the bridge ... but before it got to the bridge it disappeared ..."

This witness described this mystery animal as being as big as a tiger, so this could have been an anomalous big cat report and not a Black Dog, but that theory is belied by the sudden disappearance of the animal, a feature not often noted in Alien Big Cat (ABC) stories.

The apparition's locomotion is also odd in this account. Most often, we hear of the Black Dog walking or running like a normal animal somewhere near the percipient. The jumping and gliding movement is unusual and seems to be an outlier in the annals of our phantom.

One of my favourite stories of the Black Dog is not a favourite because of the story so much as the age of the witness. This account comes from a man who was ninety-seven years old at the time he told it to Ivan Bunn. The witness harked back to 1897 in Diss, Norfolk, for his encounter.

It was early evening and he was sitting on a stile with his girl-friend when "... something caused us to turn round ... we saw a large black dog quite close to us ... he was looking at us as if he wanted to come on over to the stile. We both jumped down to allow him to come over but he had vanished ... there was no dog in sight. We only saw him for a split-second, he was of the retriever type – rough coated – we noticed chiefly his large brown eyes."

This is one of those stories that skeptics will shrug off. Obviously, they would say, this man saw a dog, and it tucked itself off someplace while he and his lady friend weren't looking.

I beg to differ. This man told his story in 1977, and the events occurred in 1897. This gentleman had carried this event in his memory for eighty years!

Amongst all the other events of a long and presumably eventful life, a life that had spanned both world wars, this elder carried this story with him, and it still had enough impact for him to want to share it with a folklorist.

Something about this Dog made a strong impression on this fellow even though the dog seems to have been quite normal. This is a circumstance where one might wish for more detail. What was it about this animal that made such a lasting impression?

I note, too, that this Dog amongst many others seems to have evinced the Black Dog Stare reported earlier. A stile is an arrangement of steps that allows people but not animals to climb over a fence or a wall. What was it about this creature's regard that made this couple move aside so that the Dog could climb out of a place that was designed to contain him?

Let's go now to the *Shuckland* website and the testimony of F. W. Kent. Mr. Kent was working as a warrener (gamekeeper) and had been setting traps with a colleague. The two were going home along Barham Church Lane at Barham near Ipswich, Suffolk. The time was about ten in the evening, and the duo had just passed the Barham Hall gates when they saw "a large dog lying in the middle of the road".

The witness describes the Black Dog as rough-coated, about two and a half feet high (30 inches) with big, luminous eyes.

Kent struck at the creature with a stick, but the stick went right through it. He notes that had this been an ordinary dog, the blow might have killed it.

The Dog bounded away down the lane, crossed the main road and disappeared into a solid brick wall.

Black Dogs do seem to have a habit of disappearing into things. They have been seen to disappear into gravestones, cairns, hedges, and trees. Police Constable Stonehouse found that he had not been looking at an ordinary dog when he realized that the animal had moved through a solid iron gate.

Shuckland also gives us this interesting account submitted to the site by a witness' wife.

The gentleman was walking up a narrow lane near Garveston Church in Norfolk (as previously noted, churches are common sighting locations). Suddenly, he saw a large dog about twenty yards in front and to the left of his line of travel. Next to the dog was a large open field with no hedge.

The husband looked over at a woman coming from the opposite direction with her two dogs, and when he looked back, the large dog had vanished. As the witness notes, "there was absolutely nowhere it could have gone in that second, just open field with no crop. It must have vanished as it was about level with the other dogs ..."

The dog in question was described as "a 'natural' dog, with a very dark shaggy coat, but with an unusually round face for a large dog. It looked neither to right nor left, just trotting along occasionally lifting its head. It took no notice of the approaching dogs, or of anyone". The animal was about the size of a Labrador but was stated to have a head more like a boxer.

The frustrated witness noted that the creature would have had to clear two hundred yards to find any sort of cover. "Natural" dogs, even sighthounds, are not able to run that kind of distance in the time it takes one to look at another person and then look back. The witness also noted that he did not ask the woman what she saw since he did not know her and was, presumably, afraid of ridicule.

Unlike the previous story, this Black Dog seemed to take no note of the witness or of the other person and their dogs coming down the lane. We have noted that the Black Dog seems to have a good bit of agency. When I see stories where the Dog pays no regard to the witness, I wonder if that particular phantom isn't just off to another place and another witness.

A. A. MacGregor in his *The Ghost Book* gives the account of a witness walking to his home near the Ditchingham, Norfolk, railway station. He was on the road to the train station in early autumn of 1938, and the local church tower clock had just struck 2200 hours when he noted a "black shape" coming toward him at a range of about seventy-five yards. As the shape drew closer, he noted that it was "a large black dog" about 28–30 inches tall. The beast had a "long, black, shaggy coat" and was ambulating down the same side of the road as the witness.

The man moved into the centre of the road to allow the dog to pass, but as the animal pulled even with him, "it just vanished". As you might expect, the man spent several minutes searching around the area and looking over the hedge into an empty meadow before he "suddenly felt frightened, and hastened home". Despite his relatives telling him about the local Black Dog lore, the witness continued to use that route home and reportedly never had another encounter.

Shock does strange things to people. Some witnesses, seeing a creature vanish before their eyes, would have an immediate fear reaction and look for the nearest bolthole. This witness had to explore the area and make sure the Dog had actually vanished before the strangeness of his situation set in and he felt fear.

I think it is also interesting that the witness, despite his scare, continued to use that route and never had another experience. Researchers often wonder why it is that some people have one experience and never again have anything odd happen to them, while others seem to be strangeness magnets and suffer multiple events.

Anything I might say on that matter would be pure conjecture, but speaking of multiple encounters, here's a story that will make the reader wonder about the possibility that some Black Dog sightings are psychic events, a possibility discussed in chapter 26.

In the book *Apparitions*, Celia Green and Charles McCreery give the account of a woman who, while riding a bicycle home from a job serving at "T. Hall" (the authors note that this might be Toftrees Hall in the Fakenham area of Norfolk) at 2330 hours had an encounter with an "enormous" Black Dog that ran along beside her, with its tongue lolling out, and then vanished. This happened on an open road in the area of a section of woodland locally known as Bluebell Wood.

Strange, yes, but even stranger is the witness' statement that a month later, exactly, "in the same place and same time, she saw the dog again", and it behaved in exactly the same manner. Despite her love for dogs, the witness said that she "didn't feel like trying to touch the dog", so one sees again the anti-reaction that seems so often to accompany the Phantom Black Dog.

There were no further incidents until "several months later" as the witness was waiting for her sixteen-year-old daughter to return from work at a local theatre. As she stood at the gate of her home, "she saw the girl approach, but the same enormous dog was right in front of the bicycle. She was afraid that it would knock her daughter off, but as the girl got closer, the dog just vanished".

What made this account unique was that the sixteen-year-old saw and heard nothing at all, leaving one to consider how it is that the mother could see the Dog and the daughter could not. As I've mentioned previously, and will discuss in some detail later, it's quite possible that this Dog was appearing to the witness' psychic ability and not to their physical eyes.

In reading about mediums and other people with clairvoyant talent, these people often claim that, particularly when they were young, they had difficulty telling a psychic vision from what others think of as the real world. I think this might be true in the case of someone who has a spontaneous psychic event. Such a person would have no training in discerning one world from the other, so the vision of a Black Dog would look like a "real" dog.

To wind up this section, Mark Norman tells the tale of witness Nikki Hatch, who reported the following strange tale to him:

I grew up in Liphook ... My mother was in the habit of walking the dogs in the early evening around dusk. It was one such evening and I was in a pushchair so I guess I would have been about 2 or 3 years old (1965/6). The poodles apparently stopped at the crossroads ... Staring towards the right turn and growled. I remember seeing a large black dog. It's [sic] mouth was very red. It's [sic] coat was rough and coarse. It just stood looking down at me. I apparently said to my mother "Mummy, I don't like that black dog". She could see nothing. I remember it felt threatening although, to my recollection it did nothing ... My mother tells me that she saw a black dog herself only a short distance along the same path. It was standing on the path looking towards her. She bent to pick up the poodles and it was gone although she couldn't see where it could have jumped without her noticing.

Like the Dog Lane story earlier, one of the witnesses could

see the Dog and the other could not. It is doubtful whether the mother in this story would have believed the story of a two or three-year-old if she had not also had an experience herself.

Again, it is striking that something about the Phantom Black Dog impresses itself on the memory. In one account, a man carried the memory of a sighting for eighty years, and, in another, a woman who was barely old enough to have a memory carried the image of a Black Dog with her from 1965/6 to the time of her interview with Mark Norman. Again, one must ask what it is about the creature that makes such an indelible imprint on its witnesses? In both cases, the witnesses do not even report the paranormal glowing eyes, but, nevertheless, these incidents stuck with the witness for extended periods of time.

Now that the ability of the Phantom Black Dog to seemingly disappear at will and be invisible to some people but not others has been well established, we can move on to the stories of people who have tried to physically interact with a Black Dog to no avail.

18

NO TOUCHING ALLOWED

M. V. Dahlgren, in *South Mountain Magic*, tells several stories of the Snarly Yow, that Maryland area's Black Dog. This beast appears in other sections of the book, but in one story, a local claims to have seen the Black Dog "in the Gorge, just below the spring, and threw a cane at it, which seemed to not hit it, but to go right through ..."

You might be reminded of the story of Mrs. GB and her umbrella attack in the previous section, only, in this case, there is no record of the Dog disappearing. This short story is also notable since it comes to us from the US.

We move back over the Atlantic for another insubstantial Black Dog story. This tale comes from Ireland and D. A. McManus in his book *The Middle Kingdom*. In Redcross, County Wicklow, a woman identified as Margo encountered a Black Dog. The circumstances of her walk are not made clear, but, given what is known of the Black Dog, it can be surmised that the lady was on her way home from somewhere.

In any case, the beast appeared and began to trot next to her in the manner that we have seen so often, and Margo decided that it must be a good doggie and attempted to pat it. Her hand flowed right through the creature. Not to be put off, Margo tried to put her hand on the Dog "several" times with no success before being convinced that it was, indeed, a phantom and leaving it be.

This account is an example of the sometimes odd reactions people have to paranormal phenomenon. It would seem, if one had seen one's hand pass through a seemingly solid creature, that the normal reaction might be fear or at least trepidation. In this case, however, the witness seemed happy to try again and again before giving up and walking on.

We are not told how Margo felt about this sighting, but her reaction seems atypical since, despite the oddity of the incident, she does not seem extraordinarily alarmed.

As has been noted, the Black Dog is often seen beside or crossing roadways. It seems almost inevitable, then, that the Dog might get in the way of a car. We saw one example of this in the story of the RAF officers coming off Coltishall Bridge who had to brake suddenly to avoid hitting a Black Dog in the section on the Black Dog Stare.

In another account that involved a military person, given to the *Shuckland* website, we have an apparent collision:

In the Spring of 1962 I was on leave from my unit in Aden. About 00:30 hours on a Monday I was returning from a visit to London driving along the then A11 across Roudham Heath near Thetford. As I got near the point where the Peddar's [sic] Way crossed the A11 I saw a huge Newfoundland dog coming from the left along the Path. [Map Ref. TL934871]

I felt unable to do anything to avoid the dog. However there was no crash, instead the dog reappeared on my right continuing his journey. At this time I had never heard of "Old Shuck". But I knew the dog was not of this world. When I got home my mother got up to let me in and said that my hair was on end and my face as white as snow. When I told her what had happened, she said that I had seen "Old Shuck".

As an odd end note, the witness seems to feel that this encounter sparked clairvoyance in him. He says that he has "seen much of the other world" and has been able to "foresee family deaths and the illness of friends".

Given the end note, one has to wonder if the whole encounter was not some sort of psychic manifestation or initiation, perhaps the first awakening of an incipient clairvoyant talent. Not all psychics are found sitting in back rooms at the local metaphysical store; some of them may be found in uniform, like this fellow.

We might also wonder if the energy of the Black Dog or some other aspect of this sighting was, indeed, what awakened this witness' psi abilities. If a knock on the head can do it (Peter Hurkos), then I see no reason why an encounter with an apparition might not provide the shock that manifests psi. Spiritualists and magical practitioners have practiced "psychic development" for years, theorizing that the natural psi that we have as children is programmed out of us by Western scientific materialist education. If this is true and those abilities have simply gone dormant, then it seems logical that an encounter with the Other might waken them.

It is quite odd enough that our subject seems to disappear at will and be insubstantial unless it wishes to be otherwise, but we also find that there are a whole series of accounts in which the Black Dog is not visible at all. I have serious reservations about these stories since the percipient cannot see what they are encountering, but they are included since they are an oft-referenced subset of Black Dog tales.

Ethel Rudkin gives us the story of Mr. M of Willoughton in the folklorist's home province of Lincolnshire. Mr. M was secretary to the man who owned the village and was not a country person. He owned a scrappy cairn terrier that he took out for a walk each night.

On the night in question, the normally doughty terrier refused to walk past a certain spot and had dug in so that Mr. M had to put a leash on the dog and drag him past the spot that had spooked him. Mr. M freed his dog once they were past the obstruction, and the animal fled for home, something he had never done before.

"Mr. M followed and was shutting the gate when he was forced on to the gate post by something pushing on his shoulders from the front ..." He later told his wife that the sensation was of a large dog, like an Alsatian (German shepherd), with its front paws on his shoulders.

As the witness was a stranger to the village, he had never heard of the numerous Black Dog legends in the area until he spoke with Rudkin about his story. Interestingly, the events of this account take place on October 31, the Celtic feast of Samhain, and a time when the Veil Between the Worlds is supposed to be thin. Perhaps, in this case, the Veil was thin enough to allow the city boy to have a decidedly country spook experience. Or it might be that some phantom took umbrage at him dragging his dog around by the neck and decided to mete out a little paranormal justice.

Enid Porter tells a more sinister story set on Christmas Day:

One Christmas Day in the middle of the last century, Black Shuck pushed against a small blind boy who was standing with his sister on Thetford Bridge. The child asked his sister to send the big dog away, but she assured him that there was no dog anywhere near them. But he insisted that there was, exclaiming in terror that it was trying to push him into the water. Suddenly the girl felt her brother being pulled away from her, and then she knew that what he felt and what she could not see must be the dreaded Black Shuck she had so often heard about. Just in time she managed to save the little boy from over-balancing in the water then, hand-in-hand, the children raced off to their home.

While we think of Christmas as a time of good cheer, that holiday coincides with the Winter Solstice, the longest night of the year, and, in some parts of the world, not so long ago, it was a time of telling ghost stories and staying indoors to avoid the Wild Hunt.

The Solstice was also a time when the restless dead were said to walk the earth in some regional folklore. Given that the Black Dog has strong associations with death, this story fits right into the theme of longest nights and the unseen entities that inhabit them, but it does seem that the identity of this phantom comes more from local tradition than any sense of the entity itself. We've seen no clear indications that the Black Dog wishes anyone harm, just that it predicts harm.

While the Phantom Black Dog seems to impress itself on the memory, physical objects don't seem to have much effect on our subject. We have seen tales where the Dog could not be touched by hands, canes, umbrellas and sticks. In the next chapter, we will learn that the Phantom Black Dog is also not affected by firearms.

19

NO FIREARMS, PLEASE!

THERE ARE NOT a huge number of accounts where a Black Dog has been in the sights of a firearm, but such tales do exist, and several of them come from the US.

M. V. Dahlgren, in *South Mountain Magic*, gives us the story of Mr. W, a gentleman who was considered a "sure shot" and claimed to see the Snarly Yow, a Maryland Black Dog, as it crossed the road in front of him. Mr. W had his "ever-ready" rifle at hand and, "being sure of his aim", fired on the Black Dog before him. His bullet had no effect.

Not to be denied the title of Killer of Snarly Yow, Mr. W fired several more rounds after his initial shot with the same effect – the rounds went "whizzing through and through the shadow, leaving no mark".

Mr. W knew that he had met his match. "Overcome with dread", the experienced hunter fled the scene and didn't even bother to see whether Snarly Yow "retreated or pursued".

Here is another atypical reaction like the one we noted in the story of Margo in the last chapter. Once again, a person seems bound to repeat his actions around a Black Dog. Mr. W seemed to feel that one bullet, or even a couple, were not good enough. Instead, he had to fire several times before he called it quits and fled.

Could it be that the reaction of repetition is the result of people's shock at the Black Dog not being the solid animal it appears to be? Or was this case simply a matter of continuing to fire on a threat until one runs out of bullets? Either way, it becomes clear that the Black Dog is not some cryptozoological specimen to be brought to the authorities in the back of a wagon.

Alan Brown, in *Haunted Places in the American South*, speaks of an encounter with a Black Dog in the Ell Davis Woods near Eudora, Mississippi. The "boys" of three families – Oswalt, Riley and Williams – were out hunting possum when they encountered a Black Dog in the woods. The beast gave chase, and the hunters, all of them, fired "wildly" at the Dog but "were unable to hit him". The Black Dog chased them for about a mile before jumping onto a stump, letting out a "blood-curdling" howl and vanishing from view.

In a postscript to this story, Mr. Brown reports that the Dog was seen again by a man named Williams as he and his family made their way home from church. The Dog approached the wagon in which they were riding, looked at Mr. Williams, barked and disappeared. Mr. Williams died within two weeks, another example of the Black Dog as a death omen.

This Mississippi Black Dog acts atypically in the hunting story in that it does not simply cross the hunters' path or follow the hunters for some distance. This Black Dog actually chases the witnesses. Given the guardian behaviours we have seen in our subject phantom, one wonders if there was something dangerous back in those woods, something that wouldn't have been stopped by the rifles used for hunting possum.

Additionally, the Dog seems to have been seen in the depths of the forest, also not a typical behaviour for one of these road-walking phantoms.

If the Black Dog was not protecting the "boys", then what was it protecting? As previously noted, the Black Dog is known to inhabit churches, cemeteries and other sacred sites. Perhaps the "boys" stumbled upon an indigenous sacred or burial site out in those woods. This area of Mississippi is rife with aboriginal burial and sacred sites.

It is also curious that no dogs are mentioned in this tale. Possums and raccoons are most often hunted in the American South using dogs to root the prey out and tree it for the hunters. Yet we see no mention of dogs with these hunters at all. Did the canines flee in the face of their Otherworldly counterpart, or were these fellows just using hunting as an excuse to get out of the house? Or perhaps they were up to some other mischief that attracted the apparition's attention. Moonshining, perhaps?

Vance Randolph, in *Ozark Magic and Folklore*, relates the account of a close-range attempt to shoot a Black Dog. The events occurred around the town of Bunker, in Reynolds County, Missouri. Dr. J. Gordon was riding horseback and crossed a stream near a local cemetery. The good doctor was out late at night and spotted the figure of a dog, "but very much larger". The Black Dog actually "walked on water without a sound or a ripple", proving its paranormal credentials before any events transpired.

The referenced story is confusing since it states that the doctor saw this beast several times, once in "bright moonlight", so perhaps the doctor and the Dog were old acquaintances. In any event, on the night in question, the creature jumped up on the back of the doctor's horse, causing the equine to try to dislodge the apparition and the doctor both.

The physician was carrying a derringer, a small, easily concealable pistol, and emptied both barrels into his unwanted rider, "but it was not dislodged". The man then tried to hit the creature, the pistol still in his hand, but he contacted nothing and "could feel nothing ... his arm slashed right through the figure as if there was nothing there".

The animal was engaged with gunfire and then with physical blows all to no effect, and then the story ends. It is this sort of frustration with folklore that makes researchers put their head in their hands and wish for the opportunity to interview the witness themselves.

What happened after the doctor attempted to dislodge the animal? Did it jump down of its own accord? Did it hitch a ride with the doctor to the nearest crossroad and debark in a flash of light and a puff of smoke? The story is incomplete, and the principal is long in the grave, so one will never know.

Taking aim at a Black Dog is not an action confined to the States; it is also found in the accounts from south of the US border. Simon Burchell gives a good example in his book on the Black Dog in Latin America.

In 1949, "in the small village of Abadiano, in Michoacán state" (Mexico), Margarita Hernández's father had an encounter with the Black Dog (Perro Negro) of his region. The man was walking home from a vigil for his godson and had passed from the village where the vigil was held out into the flatlands that surrounded the village. A vehicle was approaching on the road, and fearing soldiers that might confiscate his pistol, the man dived over a fence and waited for the vehicle to pass.

A small black dog "appeared" before him and began to follow him despite the witness' efforts to chase it off. Ms. Hernández's father didn't know the dog and "looked around for the owner". When he turned back to the dog, he was astonished to see that it was growing in size. Notable in this encounter is the continued reference to the Black Dog staring at the witness, who became so unnerved that he drew his .38-caliber pistol.

The witness "aimed and fired, but the bullet left the gun as if in slow motion and fell intact at his feet ..." The dog had now grown to the "size of a small horse", and the terrified witness "fired again with the same result". In desperation, the witness called out to the Virgin Mary, and the creature promptly disappeared.

Before we discuss this unnerving account, let's look at another, from several thousand miles away, that also involves an odd effect on a weapon. This story comes from Ethel Rudkin and really makes one consider the advisability of firing on one of these creatures.

The story is very short and written, as was fashionable, in a semblance of the dialect of the region. "Sammy Prettle (Pretty-well, now dead) 'once shot at it [a Black Dog] ageean th' big willow tree an' is gun-barrel busted an' 'e came 'oame white as a sheet!'"

It's one thing for a weapon to have no effect on a lurking phantom but quite another to have your weapon blow up in your hand when you try to use it. One suspects that Sammy did not venture out near that willow tree anytime soon thereafter.

The Mexican account is even more off-putting since the weapon was untouched, but El Perro Negro seems to have had a type of distortion effect when the pistol was fired. The bullet exited the barrel but then simply fell to the ground. While we do not see many examples of the Black Dog having a physical effect on its environment, this incident is an important example of what happens when the phenomenon does deign to interact in our realm.

Finally, W. H. Barrett, in *East Anglian Folklore*, gives the story of a fisherman named Sam Rudd who had an encounter with a Black Dog on the beach at Salthouse, Norfolk. An impenetrable mist settled over the beach and Rudd began to hear the "baying and howling" of a dog at some distance. He fled back to his home straightaway and locked up tight behind himself, but the howling continued to disturb the peace.

Rudd's father was home at the time and took his "fowling gun", a shotgun designed for hunting birds, to the second floor of the house and threw a window open. Seeing the Black Dog sitting in the yard, the elder Rudd unloaded on the creature with a "half a pound of swan shot" with absolutely no effect.

To give an idea of the firepower brought to bear, swan shot would have about fifteen pellets per ounce, each of approximately .27 caliber. For those who might be curious, buckshot, used for hunting deer, is about .33 caliber, so this load would have had substantial impact if it had hit anything. To unload a half pound of swan shot would have required several shots being fired, again, all to no effect.

The Black Dog kept on howling, and the father went down to tell his son that it was, indeed, Black Shuck and that he was quite fortunate to have made it back into the house. When father and son went outside the next day, the only damage was to their privy door, which was riddled with shot holes.

An interesting side note to this story is that the so-called Hellhounds of Meridean Island, which were discussed earlier, were also preceded by mist that severely limited visibility. I would emphasize, too, this business of firing multiple shots at the Black Dog. It was not enough to send one load of .27-calibre projectiles at the beast; instead, the shooter had to riddle the outhouse full of holes in an effort to down the creature.

Hands and fists, canes, umbrellas, sticks and now guns. It should be obvious that the Black Dog is impervious to the sort of injury that most of us can mete out.

That fact is particularly frightening when we come to reports of Black Dogs allegedly attacking people. We examined accounts of Black Dogs killing people, and those stories seem to be dubious, but there are also a number of stories of Black Dogs supposedly causing injury to witnesses. These tales will be covered in the next section.

20

BLACK DOGS ATTACK!

THE VAST MAJORITY of legends about the Black Dog have the Dog appearing mysteriously, trotting along the side of the road for a distance, and then disappearing. No harm is done to the percipient except perhaps to their nerves. We've also shown that a Black Dog can be aggressive in its role as a guardian, as shown in chapter 16.

Of course, there are the stories of deaths following a Black Dog encounter, and it does seem that this happens more often than could be accounted for by chance. Our subject certainly can be a death portent.

In addition, there are the rare encounters where the Dog is blamed for the death of someone, although many of these cases seem dubious. What then can be made of instances where the Black Dog seems to have a physical and aggressive effect on the witness?

The most famous case of a Black Dog causing physical injury (and death) is the previously cited attack on the churches of Bungay and Blythburgh in 1577. The scorch marks on the church door at Bungay are still there, and one can see photos of them with a quick internet search. Fleming's little tract on that incident gives information on the deaths and injuries associated with that event, but it is highly likely that this account is exaggerated. The accounts of such happenings, however, are not simply confined to the Middle Ages.

Katharine Briggs, in her lengthy work on British folk tales, tells of a man who had to make the walk from Princetown to Plymouth using the road that crosses Rowborough Down. This incident takes place in Devon County, and this individual started the walk late in the day, around four o'clock. He hoped to cover the sixteen miles in three and a half hours, a very brisk pace.

It was December, "cold and frosty", and the moon was bright, providing the fellow with plenty of light to see his way. The account tells us that the man encountered no one along the way nor any animals, and he was so aware of his aloneness that he gave in to the temptation to stop at a wayside inn and have a quick drink to keep his spirits up (no pun intended).

Our witness got on his way again and was passing a copse of pine when he heard the pit-pat of feet behind him. He thought to greet his fellow traveller, but when he turned around, there was no one there. Suddenly, though, an "enormous" Black Dog appeared to his right, which he described as being like a giant Newfoundland. The man was a dog lover, so he was not overly concerned with the sight. Then, as many modern witnesses comment, things got weird:

> Presently he spoke to him. "Well, doggie, what a beauty you are; how far are you going?" at the same time lifting his hand to pat him. Great was the man's astonishment to find no resisting substance, though the form was certainly there, for his hand passed right through the seeming body of the animal. "Hulloh! what's this?" said the bewildered traveller. As he spoke the great glassy eyes gazed at him; then the beast yawned, and

from his throat issued a stream of sulphurous breath. Well, thought the man, I am in for it now! I'll trudge on as fast as legs can carry me, without letting this queer customer think I am afraid of him. With heart beating madly and feet actually flying over the stony way, he hurried down the hill, the dog never for a moment leaving him, or slackening his speed. They soon reached a crossway, not far from the fortifications, when suddenly the man was startled by a loud report, followed by a blinding flash, as of lightning, which struck him senseless to the ground. At day-break, he was found by the driver of the mail-cart, lying in the ditch at the roadside in an unconscious state.

There was a local tradition that the Dog was the ghost of a canine whose human had been murdered. The legend said that the dog ghost was "doomed to traverse this road and kill every man he encounters, until the perpetrator of the deed has perished by his instrumentality". The witness survived to tell the tale, so this legend does not seem plausible, but one does wonder what caused this poor man's injuries.

This story does give us pause. We've seen a Black Dog seemingly cause a gun barrel to burst and bullets to drop to the ground after exiting the barrel of a gun. If the apparition also has the power to strike someone down, is if with lightning, the query then would be: why?

It does not seem that this poor fellow did anything more than try to pat the nice dog he met on the road. Suddenly, however, it seems that his physical well-being is in danger.

We can conjecture about this Black Dog's motivations for an aggressive response, but we can never really know what provoked the action or even if it had anything to do with the Black Dog. Although it is supposed to have been a clear night, weather changes, and it certainly sounds like this unfortunate, who was walking out in the open on a road, might have actually been struck by lightning.

Does a Black Dog have the power to do such a thing? There is really no way to know, but as a final thought, I will mention the legend that Black Dogs are associated with storms.

Ruth Tongue, in her book of forgotten folk tales, tells a Black Shuck story that falls into our area of interest. The tale was told to Tongue in 1955 by the great-grandson of a man who came from Potter Heigham around Dovercourt, Essex.

The great-grandfather drove a cart carrying fish, bread and other goods for the farms of the area. The great-grandson notes that the cart driver endeavoured to travel during the day or to overnight safely because of bad road conditions. The cart driver also confessed that he did not like to be out after dark due to the things that haunted the lanes.

The worst of those haunts was, of course, the Shuck, a species of Black Dog encountered in these pages before. The Shuck was a thing not discussed, even by the tale teller's father, but was described as the size of a calf or donkey with eyes that lit up like lamps.

The great-grandfather had reason to fear the Shuck:

One time in early Winter the great-grandfather had been delayed, and was travelling fast for home in the moonlight when "something black" jumped out of a hedge, trying to get into the back of the cart. "The pony ran like hell and my great-granddad he yells and takes just one look and there sitting behind him all among the fish and breathing in his ears was the Black Shuck."

The cart streaked on, overturning when it couldn't take the next corner, and the witness was pitched out, falling unconscious beside the road. His son and brothers came looking for him at daylight, and although he was alright, the cart was wrecked, and the pony limped home, never doing a day's work afterwards.

Now, one might argue that the Black Dog simply spooked the cart pony when it leapt into the back of the cart, thus causing the accident. The Shuck did not technically harm either the man or the pony, but, given the previous account, where a man was seemingly struck unconscious by a Black Dog, one is given to wonder if the man's loss of consciousness was caused by the accident or the phantom.

Finally, from the *Shuckland* website, we have a more modern story that bears some resemblance to the tale of the fish cart earlier in that the Dog was not more guilty in spirit than in form. This account occurs in the village of Foulden in the Berwickshire area of the Scottish Borders:

> While staying at his grandparent's house in the village in 1997 or '98, a boy aged 6 or 7 was cycling up and down the lane which ran behind this and other houses, with a field beyond it. As he began cycling back to the house, he was terrified by a large black dog which ran after him. The gate to the house, which had been open, was now shut, and the boy crashed into it, at which point the dog vanished in front of him. The witness later described his feeling of "pure terror", and that the incident will haunt him forever.

It's certainly possible that the open gate that was then closed had a mundane explanation, but we will see poltergeist-style activity attributed to a Black Dog in Chapter 23, so the Dog might have had a hand in closing that gate.

In either event, this account also bears three other aspects of the Black Dog phenomenon that are seen repeatedly: the unreasoning terror that the sighting provokes, the indelible imprint that these creatures make in the mind of the witness, and the sudden disappearance of the animal once the incident reaches its denouement.

If we can say anything about the Black Dog after examining a number of stories, it seems to be that, where the Dog is found, strangeness follows. By itself, this fact could be very disquieting, but we have more high strangeness to explore as we consider stories of the Black Dog changing shape and size.

21

SHAPE CHANGER

ONE OF THE interesting associations that we find in Black Dog lore is the idea of the Black Dog as a shape-shifter. Theo Brown reminds us, in speaking about the many variant forms of the Black Dog, that some of those legendary variations have other forms as well as taking the shape of an enormous Black Dog. These variations include the Shuck, which is said to be able to appear as a goat, calf or horse. Suffolk's Moddey Dhoe (or Moddy Dhu) is said to have a human form (as is the Shuck). Yarmouth's Scarfe appears as a big black goat, while the Yorkshire Barguest appears as a pig, donkey or calf. Wakefield's Padfoot takes the unusual appearance of a calf with twisted spiral horns, which can also be white or yellow.

Brown also clues us into the fact that the legends report Black Dogs with two heads, no head or one eye in the middle of the forehead.

We saw an instance of a Black Dog seemingly shifting into a bipedal donkey, and as we will discuss in a moment, there are examples of witnesses being unsure what they were looking at, so it is possible that our phantom can change form, in addition to all the other high strangeness around it. At that point, however, are we even dealing with a Phantom Black Dog? If so, how would we identify the new creature as a Shuck or other variant if we did not see the creature change? I can't answer that question, and I expect that the folklorists would be hard-pressed to do so.

While folklore is rife with legends of the werewolf, a person who can transform into a wolf, I found it interesting that there is also one legend of a person changing into a Black Dog and back, all in one legendary account. There is some argument about where this story first appeared, but Enid Porter tells a version:

On occasions Shuck could take on human form. A tale was told around Lowestoft of a dark-complexioned stranger who suddenly appeared in the neighbourhood; an Italian, people said he was, although he spoke English well. He became friendly with a fisher boy whom he tried to persuade to accompany him to "foreign parts". The lad, however, refused, so the stranger, telling him that he himself had to go, asked him to look after a large black dog, a dog which had been seen about the place since the Italian's arrival though never, people had noticed, with his master.

The boy consented, the stranger left and soon the dog and its new owner were inseparable, often swimming together in the sea. One fateful day, however, the lad swam far out to sea and when he turned round to come back to the shore, he was horrified to find that the dog would not allow him to do so, but with horrible growling and snapping at his legs and neck compelled him to go farther out to sea, the dog keeping close behind him. The plight of the poor lad was terrible in the extreme, and a fearful death confronted him.

On, on he swam, and ever behind him swam the much-dreaded Black Shuck. So frightened was he that he dared no [sic] turn his head to look at the beast, but at length he heard the panting and growling of the dog by his side and, turning his head, he was horrified to see, not the shaggy head of the dog but the head and saturnine face of the Italian. He bestowed upon the boy a hellish and triumphant grin, and then instantly resumed the form of the dog and again "flew" at his neck with a savage snarl. Just as the boy felt that he must sink, a sailing-ship passed within hearing distance, and he was hauled aboard, his neck fearfully lacerated by the dog's teeth. The animal dived like a whale and was seen no more ...

This sounds more like a "cautionary tale" urban legend than a witness account, and Simon Sherwood notes that the account appears in other sources but sporting a different town name. Nevertheless, it is an interesting tale, and one wonders if the prevalence of werewolf lore throughout Europe did not find a small foothold in the legends of the Black Dog in Britain. This tale of a Black Dog / human shape-shifter is the only such example, other than the brief mention of Moddey Dhoe (Suffolk) having a human form, found in the research for this book.

Another notable example of bending the laws of nature that we see with the Phantom Black Dog is the notion that the phantom can change its size. Speaking specifically of Black Shuck, one will recall the tale of the talking Black Dog that predicted a man's death, "I shall be wanting you within the week ..." The dog is also noted to have grown in size as it blocked the man's path before his unfortunate demise two days later.

We also saw this unusual characteristic in the Snarly Yow story from Dahlgren that appears in chapter 4. In that story, a man returning from making some purchases at a local store found his path blocked by the Black Dog of his area. In that account, the man tried to fight the beast. Not only did his blows have no effect at all, but the creature actually grew in size as he tried to get it to move out of his path.

In both these stories, the Black Dog was blocking a road and preventing someone from passing. It may be that the Dog got larger to prevent that passage. It is frightening enough to have one's way blocked by a larger-than-average dog, but when you add in the glowing eyes and size variance, I would think that would be quite enough to hold a person in place for whatever length of time the Dog might deem necessary. As we saw in chapter 4, these apparitions that are holding people in place may actually be doing them a favour.

Lon Strickler, in a *Phantoms and Monsters* blog dated 20 March 2019, gives us a more modern size-shifting account:

> My god-daughter who is 18 saw something last year that I can't get off of my mind. She and her best friend were in a neighborhood in New Oxford, Pennsylvania. They were in a car just talking. My god-daughter looks up and sees what she thought was a dog sitting near an electrical box. She didn't see a lot of details. She says it was black. All black. She could see black eyes that she noticed because of street lights. Then, she says it noticed her looking at it and it "expanded." I asked her to elaborate. She said it grew twice its size and started running at the car. Both girls saw this, screamed and hauled out of there. My god-daughter said it ran beside the car for a bit then disappeared. She felt sick as well after it was over.

The reporting person states that the Dog was built like a Great Dane and, as an interesting side note, states that the goddaughter and her best friend's relationship disintegrated after this sighting. It seems that any "disaster" that befalls a witness after sighting one of these beings is automatically assigned to the agency of the Black Dog.

Given the ongoing social ups and downs of teenagers, the phantom may have caused this falling-out, the two may have argued over other pressures in their relationship, or, as can be seen in some witnesses, the breakup may have been caused by something as simple as one party wanting to discuss the matter and the other trying to forget it happened.

The interesting part of this story to me is that the Black Dog changed shape as soon as it noticed that it was being watched and then continued to grow as it charged the car and then followed the vehicle for a short while. This incident seems to be an example of the Black Dog being territorial, but these territorial displays often seem to be associated with the guardian behaviour. We might also consider what sort of neighbourhood these two girls were in and what they were up to at the time.

We've seen several examples where the Black Dog seems aggressive but then turns out to be acting to prevent human injury, and the Dog seems to have a particular soft spot for young women.

There are examples in Black Dog lore where the witness was not, at first, sure what they were looking at. For example, D. A. McManus' tale of his friend who was treed by a Black Dog next to a river in Ireland begins with the witness thinking he was looking at an enormous panther. Later in the book, you will meet the Ozark Howler, a creature that some say looks more like a Black Dog and others claim looks like a black panther or Alien Big Cat from Britain.

Noted Fortean researcher Nick Redfern, writing in his book *There's Something in the Woods*, tells the story of Ronda, a woman who encountered a distinctly odd Black Dog in the Palo Duro State Park in Texas. Ronda, her daughter, and son-in-law had travelled to the park, a short distance from Amarillo, and had then walked into a natural area of the park before pulling out a picnic basket for lunch.

As sometimes happens in paranormal incidents, the witness had "a sudden and eerie feeling". The feeling was strong enough to compel Ronda to turn about, at which time she spotted a Black Dog that she later described as "half as large again" as a large German shepherd. The animal had dark colouring and appeared to be looking intently at the witness at a range of about two hundred feet.

The Dog did not do anything unusual at first, simply standing its ground and watching as any canine might when its territory was questioned. The behaviour changed abruptly when Ronda tried to turn her back on the beast.

The animal charged to within fifty feet, growling, barking, and snapping in a very aggressive way. Even more eerie, the dog's eyes "seemed to glow silver, not like normal eyes". To round out the paranormal nature of the animal, Ronda stated that the Dog seemed to bounce into the air "like it was on springs". When Redfern asked for clarification, she said that it simply went up and then dropped down with no evident effort from its legs.

To round out the lunchtime strangeness, Ronda states that the animal appeared to take on the shape of a "humungous black panther" at one point. The trio of picnickers had seen quite enough and vacated the area as quickly as possible. The Black Dog followed the entire way until the group reached a re-creation of a teepee (tipi) at which point the animal vanished before their eyes.

This story contains a number of Black Dog elements – size, eyes, the Stare and territoriality – but it also harks back to the Barguest and its friends in Britain, which appeared as Black Dogs when they liked and as other creatures when they chose. The idea of the Black Dog as a shape-shifter makes for interesting conjecture. Recall the story in chapter 6 where a Black Dog disappeared into a bush and blackbirds were driven out of the bush moments later. That incident could be sheer coincidence, but, then again, it might not be!

There have been a few accounts in these pages where a Black Dog has either first appeared to be a black panther or has taken on that appearance, as in Ronda's story. The UK and the US, both homes of the Phantom Black Dog, also have strong folkloric and witness evidence of out-of-place big cats. The British have even given their felines the designation Alien Big Cat or ABC. ABC reports, like those of the Black Dog, continue to come in, to the present time.

We have seen a story where a human turned into a Black Dog, and we have seen several tales where the Black Dog changed size and even shape. In the next section, the Dog will shift again, this time to bipedal locomotion, a topic that brings us into contact with modern-day cryptozoology.

22

TWO LEGGER

OF COURSE, when one thinks of Black Dogs wandering about on their back legs, one has to wonder if there is any relation between the Black Dog and the Manwolf sightings that have become so common in recent years. Linda Godfrey's work on that phenomenon has boomed over time, moving from the regional Beast of Bray Road to encompass a flood of sightings that have been sent to Ms. Godfrey from locations all over the world.

In the British lore, the Black Dog is almost exclusively quadrupedal, but Mark Norman does mention the presence of upright Black Dogs being reported at Newton St. Cyres in Devon and also at the London Borough of Islington on the road to Lenda Farm. Unfortunately, there is no further information given about these sightings, so it is difficult to draw any suppositions.

We also have the 1908 sighting, in chapter 4, of a Black Dog that then morphs into a bipedal donkey, but that account falls more into the shape-shifting realm despite the creature's display of bipedalism.

When we turn to more modern times, however, we find the

following intriguing account on the Shuckland website, from the early 2000s:

In the early 2000s, two witnesses were walking on Gunton Cliffs, having left a park (presumably the nearby Pleasurewood Hills Theme Park), when they saw a black dog running on its hind legs towards the park. Although it was a misty night, they could see it was about seven feet (2.1 meters) tall, with a small head compared to its body, and glowing yellow eyes the size of coffee mugs. The dog apparently paused, looked at them, then continued running away towards the park.

Now, I might be willing to put this down to the more modern-day phenomenon of the Manwolf but there are a couple of Black Dog trademarks in this account – the eyes glow, they are the size of coffee mugs, and this apparition manifests the stare that I expounded on in Chapter 13. The Dog is black, and it is enormous, but we see this in some of the Manwolf stories as well, particularly in the smooth-coated Anubis-type home invaders that Ms. Godfrey sets in an almost separate category.

What makes me suspect that these two men, in the Suffolk region, were seeing a Black Dog walking on two legs is the description of the head. One of the things that seems to set Ms. Godfrey's Manwolves apart is the very consistent description of the ears as being upright, like those of a wolf, jackal, or German shepherd. This feature is something that witnesses, from many different locales, seem to latch on to in their reports, and I do not see it in this description.

If the Phantom Black Dog can disappear, be unaffected by firearms and change shape and size, amongst other fascinating effects, I see no reason why it cannot walk on two legs as well.

Linda Godfrey might even agree with me. In *Monsters of Wisconsin*, she notes the following:

> Dogs that guard an island are also part of the lore of Okauchee Lake in Waukesha County, according to a musician named Scott who spent his childhood summers at an aunt's cottage on the western shore of the lake. The cottage was near an island with the ruins of an old mansion. Area residents believed the mansion's grounds were patrolled by red-eyed, black dogs that walked upright, but Scott never dared to go find out for himself if the legend was true. His family called the isle Haunted Island.

Here is a classic Black Dog setup – the location is near water, and, in other notes, Godfrey tells the reader that there once was an "ancient, thirty-foot diameter conical burial mound as well as other sites sacred to Native Americans". The fact that this site may be "patrolled" by Black Dogs should be no surprise to those who have read this far, but the idea that they walked upright while doing so does give one pause.

If UFOs can evolve from the airships of the 1800s to the Tic Tacs of today, is it not possible that the Black Dog is trying to up its game as well? That idea certainly seems to be the case in this account from Jason Offutt's *From the Shadows* blog.

The witness, S. Costea, lived in the area of Romulus, Michigan (interesting since the Romulus of legend was raised by a she-wolf) with his mother, her significant other and the boy's uncle. Their house was separated from the road by a dense swath of forest, and the witness claimed that something frightening lived there – a Black Dog with glowing red eyes.

The creature was the size of a Great Dane, and Costea described the beast as very "werewolf-like", though he does not elucidate this statement. As I've noted previously, people who have no familiarity with the Black Dog lore often fall back on the term "hellhound" to describe what they saw, but there is another witness statement, in the next chapter, where an apparition that is plainly a Black Dog is described as a werewolf. When one is faced with the unknown, my thought is that people will use descriptors with which they are familiar.

In any event, everyone who lived in the house knew about the animal, and the uncle tried throwing things at it to make it depart. It would rear up on its hind legs and charge a short distance toward the man.

While the "dog creature" did not harm the human residents of the house, chickens and rabbits seemed to be fair game "after thunderstorms" (another but very tenuous storm association). The household knew the predator was the dog thing because of the prints it left in the mud and claw marks on the window ledges, an interesting deviation from the normal Black Dog that leaves no sign.

Eventually, the creature focused on the house, tearing screens off of windows and ripping the metal mesh out of screen doors. The situation got worse when the dog creature turned its attention to Costea himself:

One summer night my mom had left the window open in my bedroom to cool the room off so I could sleep," Costea said. "She was on her way to the bathroom and went by my room and heard me talking to someone." Stopping by her son's door, well after his bedtime, she thought he was playing. She opened the bedroom door, turned on the lights, and saw the dog. "When she opened the door she saw me standing in my bed and I had apparently wet my pajamas," he said. "I was talking towards the window. I wasn't screaming or freaking out but seemed to be transfixed and talking in a low voice towards the window."

Costea didn't notice his mother, nor did he notice the tungsten light that suddenly poured a yellow glow through the bedroom. His focus was on what was at the window. "When she looked towards the window the dog had its two front paws pushed through the screen and was looking through the window at us and making a low growl," Costea said. "Its eyes glared red." Costea's mother threw the beer bottle she carried into the beast's face. Startled, it backed out of the window. She slammed the window shut and closed the blinds.

One would hope that this would be the end of the incident, but it was not. Costea acted in a very uncharacteristic manner for a little over a week after the event. He would say things that made no sense to his mother, prick his fingers with any sharp object he could find, and paint with his blood on the walls.

His very presence in a room seemed to scare the life out of the cats. Apparently, his energy at the time did not mesh with that of the felines, and they avoided him as if he were hunting them. The aversion of the cats is an interesting feature since there is extensive lore stating that both cats and dogs are able to see some of the creatures of the Otherworld.

John Michael Greer, in his book on monsters and monster investigation, emphasizes that investigators should pay attention to the reaction of dogs and cats to any phenomenon being reported. As well, there are ghost-hunting teams and even Sasquatch investigators who are experimenting with the use of dogs to help them with their hunts. It makes sense that a creature with superior senses to a human being might be sensitive to cues to which humans are blind.

In addition to all these other issues, lights burned out regularly in the home, and the whole family noted a strong septic smell in the home, a classic sign of a hostile haunting.

Oddly, the "haunting" came to an end when Costea's uncle

tired of the constant presence of the "dog creature" and shot at it with a .22 rifle. The beast fled into the forest after shots were fired and was not seen again, a marked difference between this creature and the classic Black Dog, which, we have seen, shrugs off bullets or simply doesn't allow them to leave the barrel.

In this case, we have a Black Dog, massive with the normal glowing red eyes, but behaving in a completely abnormal manner. It is not haunting a road (though there was one nearby), it is showing a bluff charge behaviour similar to that seen in Manwolves, and it is seen on its hind legs. On top of its other abnormal behaviour, the beast is accused of preying on livestock and even leaving physical signs.

In addition, there are also elements of a hostile haunting in this story along with what sounds like a near possession. Ethel Rudkin and Theo Brown would not have recognized this creature as their beloved Black Dog, but, as I mentioned at the beginning of the tale, it is just possible that the apparition could be evolving in this age of interest in the paranormal.

As noted earlier in the book, I very seldom use the term demon or demonic, and when I do use that term, it is within very narrow parameters that I will discuss later in the book. We've seen no lore suggesting that a Black Dog ever attempted to possess someone, so I wonder if S. Costea and his family didn't happen to settle near what John Keel called a "window area".

This case seems to have elements of the Black Dog story in it along with elements of demonic obsession / attempted possession. I discuss demons – how to define them and their role or lack of it in the Black Dog phenomenon – in the final section of the book.

In regard to the Black Dog elements of this account, we have no idea what happens when we, cumulatively, turn our attention to a phenomenon. Perhaps, we are providing an impetus for that phenomenon to change. I will be interested in seeing whether the coming years will bring more bipedal Black Dogs stories and how those will interrelate with the stories of the Manwolf.

This account is quite compelling even though it is not a classic Black Dog tale. The Costea tale serves as a transition. During my research, obviously, I was looking for accounts that fit into the classic patterns seen in the folklore. As the reader can see from the earlier chapters, that search was very successful. Now, however, it is time to move more toward the fringe of this fringe subject.

23

RANDOM ODDITIES

BEFORE CLOSING this section on the many strange aspects of Black Dog lore, I have to note that some of the stories encountered in the research did not fit neatly into the chapter titles derived for this book. However, as with all things paranormal or Fortean, there are always outliers, stories that may be the exception that proves the rule or, as I noted earlier, may be signs of an evolution of the Black Dog phenomenon. Regardless, I did not feel that I could ignore these accounts simply because they did not fit neatly into one of my categories.

Simon Sherwood's *Shuckland* site quotes an earlier article that lists a frightening example of a Black Dog scaring the wits out of a young couple during World War II. This encounter took place in Walberswick, Suffolk:

> ... it was in this area, during World War Two, that he [the Phantom Black Dog] gave an American airman and his wife a night they would never forget. The couple had rented a flat-topped hut on the edge of Walberswick Marsh [Common] while the husband served at a nearby air base. One stormy

evening they were startled by a violent pounding on the door. The airman peeped through a window and saw a huge black beast battering their home.

The terrified couple piled what little furniture they had against the door, then cowered as the attacker hurled his body against first one wall, then another, then leapt onto the roof. The ordeal lasted several hours before the noise faded away. The couple waited anxiously for daylight, and at dawn crept outside to inspect the damage. There was no sign of the attack, and no paw or claw marks in the soft mud around the hut.

Other than the young serviceman seeing the Black Dog when he looked out the door to see what was pounding, this sounds almost exactly like one of those "forest poltergeist" cases, often assigned to Sasquatch, where there is repeated pounding on the walls of a home. Such racket often wakes the witnesses, and sometimes they will spot their big hairy monster.

At other times, the phantom pounder is not seen, and no trace can be found when the witnesses rise in the morning, despite instances where there are muddy flower beds and other so-called track traps around the house.

In this case, as with many others, no harm came to the witnesses other than a sleepless night, but it is definitely the case that this Black Dog seemed to have had a strong physical effect on the cottage while, at the same time, leaving no sign of its passing. The lack of paw or claw marks, tracks or other traces of the beast mimics poltergeist phenomena where items in a home can be physically displaced but whatever is causing this disarray leaves no trace of its presence.

The next account also comes from the *Shuckland* website, where Robert Harman reports from Tuckswood, the most southern suburb of Norwich, between Eaton and Old Lakenham. Harman, who lived in a house in this suburb, was reading a book about midnight on a Saturday in 1986. He heard a scratching noise from outside and went to investigate, but, finding nothing, he started back toward the house. He heard the noise again and, this time, determined that the sound was coming from behind the garden shed.

Harman looked around the side of the shed, and imagine his surprise when he encountered an enormous dog with a black coat and "big red eyes". The witness reports thinking that he was face to face with a werewolf, so sinister was the creature's gaze.

As I noted in the previous chapter, the werewolf comparison seems to be more common in modern-day sightings, where witnesses are not as aware of the lore of the Phantom Black Dog and, perhaps, fall back on themes wrested from horror television and movies.

The animal moved away from him, stopping to look back twice, and then vaulted a six-foot fence with no perceived effort. The witness was brave enough to jump up on the fence and look over. He saw the Dog walk away down the road, headed toward the countryside.

I have the image in my mind of this backyard haunting Black Dog strolling nonchalantly down the lane, off to frighten some country dweller before calling it a night. This is the only account I can bring to memory that features a Black Dog in a suburban backyard, so I found the story quite unusual.

Despite its unusual location at the time of the sighting, the Black Dog does display the characteristic big red eyes, it proceeds down a road once it is over the fence, and the witness shows the extreme fear reaction that we see in so many Black Dog reports. The witness' final note to the account is that he "hoped never to see such a creature again!"

The *Eastern Daily Press*, a regional Norfolk newspaper,

contained the following story in its Spooky Norfolk section. One "thundery evening", a young mother and her six-year-old son, who were on holiday at the Norfolk coast, found themselves looking for an open store so that they could purchase a pint of milk. When the witness finally found a place to make the transaction, she found that her son had fallen asleep in the back seat of the car and so left him for a moment to get the milk.

When the mother returned to the car, she found her son sitting, bolt upright, in the back seat of the vehicle, his face pale white. At first, the witness assumed that the child had been frightened by the booming thunder, but as she moved to enter the vehicle, she spotted "an extremely huge scruffy dog" moving away from the scene.

Checking on her son, the mother inquired as to what had scared him, and the boy replied that he had "just seen a were-wolf!" The witness tried to laugh this off, saying that the son had seen a large dog, but he insisted that the "dog" had "orange fire-balls in its eyes" and had tried to enter the vehicle.

The mother wasn't quite sure what to make of this story, but she did note that, when she was packing the car the next day, she found "big muddy paw prints on the bonnet [an American would call this the hood] and the back windows".

It's very uncommon for a Black Dog to leave physical evidence, and if it weren't for the detail of the eyes, one might be inclined to put this account down to an overly friendly, or unfriendly, canine. I found the detail of the Dog trying to enter the car particularly disturbing. Dogs, even Black Dogs, do not have hands, so what did this young one see exactly? How was the phantom trying to enter the car?

With the evidence of the eyes, the child's palpable terror, the detail of the canine trying to enter the car and the physical traces, one might conclude that something out of the ordinary happened to this young boy, and Norfolk is the prowling ground of the legendary Black Shuck, one of the less friendly varieties of Black Dog.

I have mentioned the Travel Channel show *Monsters and Mysteries in America* in the section on the Black Dog's proximity to water. In season 2, episode 5, the broadcast featured another "hellhound" story that took place in Palm Springs, California.

Palm Springs is located in the deserts of California, so the first unusual thing about this account is that it happened to be raining that night. We've mentioned the idea that Black Dogs are reputed to be linked to storms, and this account is mentioned briefly in the chapter on storms, but there is other strangeness that follows.

As noted, it was a rainy Saturday night in 2013, when Ron Palfrey wandered out to lock his front gate, a security measure that he took most nights despite his protestation on camera that the neighbourhood was safe. His attention was attracted by the sound of heavy breathing and growling, and he looked up from his gate to see two animals unlike anything he had ever seen before.

Palfrey described the beasts as looking like wolves, only larger than any wolf, with the glowing red eyes characteristic of the Black Dog. The witness experienced the fear reaction that is so often seen in the presence of these apparitions and ran back into his home, locking the door behind him and telling his wife immediately. There is no indication in the report that his wife saw the animals.

These dark wolfy animals are odd enough, but the size of these beasts makes one recall that dire wolves, a larger and heavier version of today's *Canis lupus*, were native to this region but died off somewhere between ten and sixteen thousand years ago. A mere drop in the bucket of geological time.

If it were not for the detail of the glowing red eyes, a sure sign of the Phantom Black Dog, this could have been a relict example of that species. As witnessed, one wonders if the creatures could have been spectres of that old species. I will deal further with the idea of Black Dogs as ghosts in the Theories section of the book.

While I am not a huge proponent of the Black Dog as a ghost (see the chapter on ghosts in the Theories section), I am also not opposed to the idea of animal spirits haunting a former locale. The only item in the report that drops this firmly into Black Dog territory is the note about the glowing red eyes. I am not sure that a ghost would manifest this way, but when dealing with the Otherworld, it is best to keep an open mind.

This account is strange enough, but the following morning, Jim Flood, Palfrey's neighbour, went out to get his morning paper and found that his vehicle had been "vandalized". He called police, and as they investigated, it became evident to them that the damage to the auto had been done by an animal.

Palm Springs residents often see coyotes in their area, but a coyote simply lacks the power to do the damage documented in the television series. In fact, there is no predator native to that region that is capable of tearing off part of the bumper of a car. This is doubly true since the beast, whatever it was, left large, canine footprints.

This case is interesting since it is one of those rare instances where the Black Dog seems to have left some physical evidence behind it. The damage to the vehicle reminded me of the damage to Tom and Mary Waye's vehicle documented in Lyle Blackburn's book on the Bishopville Monster. While the creature in Bishopville was reported to be upright and bipedal, the fang marks and obvious strength of that monster seem to rival the accused Black Dog in this incident.

Palm Springs is not the only American locale with an interesting "hellhound".

According to the website *Ozark Howler Info*, the Ozark Mountain region of the US has its own strange critter, dubbed the Ozark Howler. Witnesses describe the beast as the size of a bear with horns and a shaggy black coat. The creature is said to make a sound somewhere between a wolf's howl and the bugle of an elk.

As sometimes happens in Britain, where Black Dogs get mixed in with Alien Big Cats, the Howler has been described as both a dog and cat. One wonders if the Howler isn't closer kin to the Appalachian region Wampus Cat than to our current subjects, but at least some of the witness accounts seem to match the Phantom Black Dog.

A witness named Mikayla had a late-night roadside encounter with a creature that she recounts looked like a "deer and a dog had a one night stand". I can only imagine that the witness saw a dog with what appeared to be horns.

The shape-shifting varieties of Black Dog, mentioned earlier in the text, are sometimes described as having huge ears that look like horns or actually having horns. In any event, the black beast was standing on the side of the road, but Mikayla does not tell the reader if her "hellhound" had glowing eyes or not. She seemed very concerned about the idea that the creature might be a precursor of death, but there is no follow-up to the story, so one can hope that she and her relatives remained unharmed.

Another Howler witness, Nancy, from Oregon County, Missouri, wrote into the *Roundrock Journal* with her report. She recounts the story of a friend who rose at 4:30 to tend to livestock and, when he got outside, noticed that his animals were obviously frightened and huddled in a corner of the fence near his house. He had binoculars with him and, looking off in the direction from which the animals had run, spied a bizarre creature that he at first mistook for a big, black panther (the ABC connection arises again). Nancy says that the witness changed his mind as he got a better look at the animal:

> It had very long ears, or horns, and was black with thick fur. It had a long tail like a cat, but looked like a mix between a dog and a cat. It was broad and about as big as a Great Dane, and it had eerie reddish eyes that gave him chills.

Nancy winds up the story with the note that there was no reason for this person to make up such a story and that the witness was very shaken by the sighting. Reading that statement, I was immediately reminded of the farmer in *South Mountain Magic*, described in Chapter 9, whose nerves were "racked to the centre".

As I noted, the Howler's description varies from witness to witness, and this creature may be more Alien Big Cat than Black Dog, but the roadside appearances, particularly at night, the evident size of the creature, the shaggy pelt and the eerie red eyes could lead one to consider the Howler as a possible variant of the Black Dog.

As this section on the different high strangeness aspects of the Black Dog phenomenon comes to an end, I wanted to include a story that was so odd that Linda Godfrey almost did not include it in her book *I Know What I Saw*, a book of modern-day monster encounters that runs the gamut from traditional monsters to those never seen before.

The witness is Garrett Aziz, and the events of his story take place in 2015 in Lake County, California. The witness freely admitted that he used marijuana but also stated emphatically that it had never given him hallucinations. Given the details of this story, one understands why the witness inserted that proviso.

The witness was letting his dog, a Chinese Shar-Pei, out for the last time between 2230 and 2300 hours. As Garrett stargazed, he states that he felt a powerful "presence", and ten feet from where he stood on the patio was an all-black dog of tremendous size. The witness states that the dog's eyes were level with his as it stood on all fours, and the witness gave his height as five feet eight.

Now this is quite strange enough, but Garrett goes on to tell Ms. Godfrey that the dog was "absolutely psychic, or telepathic" and that he felt the beast was scanning him in some way. I found this personally interesting since the Black Dog of lore is known for its intense regard as well as its seeming agency in choosing whom to appear to and perhaps whom to protect. Perhaps this "scan" is how the Dog makes it decision. Or perhaps this psychic incursion is a new development in Black Dog lore.

Unlike other Black Dog witnesses, Garrett felt no fear, and once the enormous dog had moved off, he went to look for his Shar-Pei.

The story has a final, bizarre twist. Garrett claims that he found the enormous dog, now shape-shifted to a more appropriate size for the deed, copulating with his Shar-Pei. Being wise enough not to disturb this entity, whatever it was, he walked away, and his dog returned to him once the act was complete.

Garret went on to have an incredible dogman experience in Hawaii later in the year, but the super interesting postscript to this story is that Garrett's Shar-Pei had puppies after this unlikely encounter. Godfrey included a picture of the pups in the book, and they look quite normal, but one has to wonder if they sometimes sport glowing red eyes when Garrett is not looking.

Now, it would be easy to pass this story off as the ramblings of a drug-addled gentleman who, perhaps, put the wrong sort of mushrooms in a meal or didn't realize that his marijuana was laced with something more powerful. The trouble is that, when one begins to look at the theories behind the stories of Phantom Black Dogs, one can explain some of our phantoms with mundane explanations, but there are also whole new levels of arcana that could support even Garrett's wild story.

SECTION FOUR
THEORIES

What if we're surrounded by an ecosystem of
disincarnate consciousnesses, some of which
once inhabited physical bodies, while others
have not? Maybe riding these meat suits
around is the experiment and our interactions
with the Other merely observation of such.

Tobias Wayland
Singular Fortean Society

24

BEGINNING THOUGHTS

WE HAVE JUST SPENT a lot of time and energy looking at the Black Dog from varying angles. We have explored the classic definition of the Black Dog and some of its possible progenitors. We looked at where one might find one of these nomadic apparitions and the wonderful panoply of weirdness that surrounds this phenomenon. As I have gone through these varying chapters, I have commented on the cases as we travelled along, pointing out some of the commonalities and, more or less, typical aspects of a Black Dog case.

Now that we have spent some time in the world of the Phantom Black Dog, I want to propose some ideas about this apparition. The thing that the reader should be aware of, going into this section, is that I don't feel the need to prove anything. Due to the variable nature of this phenomenon, there is no way that we will get most of the current crop of modern scientists to pay any attention to the paranormal, Fortean or cryptozoological.

Scientists are, for the most part, academics, or they work for labs with a profit motive. The academic lives and dies by his or her writings and by having grants approved. Neither of those occupations allows time for straying into fringe topics, even if the person is so inclined, and the institutions that give grants are not amenable to research in these areas. A scientist who works in a for-profit lab is limited by what their employer says they can work on, and very few employers are interested enough in Forteana to spend money on investigating the strange.

There are exceptions to these rules, but the important point here is to realize that we don't need scientists to view the topics we are interested in as valid.

Now, I am not completely discounting science. You will find a whole chapter on mundane explanations for the Phantom Black Dog below. That chapter will be followed by several chapters that propose theories that wander from the fringe of science right off the edge into magic and animism.

I make no apologies for taking up these topics since I come at the world of high strangeness from the standpoint of animism. For those not familiar with the term, we can turn to Wikipedia for a quick definition:

> **Animism** (from Latin: anima, "breath, spirit, life") is the belief that objects, places and creatures all possess a distinct spiritual essence. Potentially, animism perceives all things – animals, plants, rocks, rivers, weather systems, human handiwork, and perhaps even words – as animated and alive. Animism is used in the anthropology of religion as a term for the belief system of many indigenous peoples, especially in contrast to the relatively more recent development of organized religion.

I have removed the footnotes from this text for clarity of copy, but the article is freely available from the source and is referenced in the bibliography.

My readers, of course, are entitled to believe anything they wish, but I want to make it clear that this Theories section will rest on several ideas that are crucial to the concepts I propose going forward.

1. There is a consensual reality in which we all live and take part. This "world" is what most people think of as real, solid and physical although even modern science (physics) agrees that it is not.

2. As noted above, all the structures of that consensual reality have a "distinct spiritual essence" – trees, plants, rocks, animals, etc.

3. In addition to the consensual, so-called physical reality, there is also a world or plane (perhaps more than one) where these essences, which we will call spirits for ease of use, live. The spirits are multitudinous in nature and range in disposition from actively helpful to humans to actively hostile to humans. This realm also includes the realm of the human dead (ancestors).

4. There have been people, throughout human history, who can, either intentionally or unintentionally, see into the Otherworld and see the spirits in this world. There are also people who, usually as a result of a calling from the spirits, have learned to interact with this world. These folks are most often referred to by anthropologists as shaman, though this term is really a cultural appropriation from the Siberian people, where the term originated.

As a sort of point 4a, there are also people in non-native cultures who work within various magical traditions and have varying levels of interaction with the spirits. Examples can be found in the modern neopagan movement, ceremonial magic, certain traditions of witchcraft and so forth.

If we can set aside our Western education, which teaches us scientific materialism from the time we are old enough to walk, and relax our minds into the animistic paradigm, we may have an easier time walking the path of the strange. Given the variability of the phenomena we study, the scientific method is not easily applicable, and "proof" will be in short supply. I will comment further on this idea in the conclusion of this work, using the craziness of Skinwalker Ranch as an example of what happens when science actually does attempt to work with the paranormal.

Animism, however, brings us closer to the heart of the extraordinary. It is useful to remember that animism is still the belief system of hundreds of thousands of people across the world. It may well be that, for whatever reason, it is the temporary experience of some of our witnesses, as well.

I have had strong shamanic leanings since my thirties (and I am sixty now), but the book that really got me thinking about the interface between our ordinary reality and the Otherworld and the porousness of that interface was John Michael Greer's *Monsters: An Investigator's Guide to Magical Beings*. In that book, a noted Golden Dawn magician (and leader of a Druid group) takes a look at legends such as vampires, werewolves, ghosts and the fae and offers a reasoned approach to dealing with such entities.

While I didn't agree with everything Greer said, I agreed with enough of his approach to change my whole view of the world of high strangeness. To reinforce that change in my world view, certain synchronicities placed me in contact with magical practitioners who had taken Greer's words to heart. Their admittedly subjective views of some of the cases they worked and hard opinions on how to stop supernatural incursions gave me yet more food for thought.

It is my hope that, as you explore the theories outlined in this section of the book, you will find some items that make you think and, maybe, even view your world differently. Remember that, while it is possible to change one's perceptions via chemical means, it is also possible to enter states of what Patrick Harpur called daimonic (not to be confused with demonic) reality using nothing but the powers of the mind.

It's essential, as we dive into theories about Phantom Black Dogs, that we take a moment to look at our thinking as well.

I've noted a tendency in paranormal, Fortean and cryptozoological research toward what I call *either/or thinking*. Either a thing must be **this** or it must be **that**. For example, there is the continuing argument in Sasquatch circles between what is called the flesh and blood hypothesis (Sasquatches are giant apes or relict hominids) and the interdimensional hypothesis (Sasquatches are beings of spirit that only exist in this realm temporarily).

I would suggest to those in their respective foxholes that it is time to declare a truce and look at our subjects with *both/and thinking*. In the case of the Sasquatch example, this would involve the acceptance, by both sides, of the validity of the other side's viewpoint, even if we don't agree with it. This would result in a lot less ink being spilled and a lot more research getting done.

My own thinking on the Sasquatch subject, for example, is that there seem to be incidents and witness accounts that would align with a physical, apelike creature but that there are also incidents and witness accounts that are so covered in high strangeness that a physical entity seems out of the question. I think we need to make space in our brains to be able to believe that both things might be true.

In light of this idea of *both/and thinking*, I am going to start off my discussion of Black Dog theories with a quick look at the more mundane explanations for our subject and then move on to a number of theories, all of which may have some bearing on our subject.

25

THE SKEPTIC'S TRIAD

IN LOOKING at mundane reasons for a witness to claim a Black Dog sighting, we have to look at something I call the skeptic's triad: misidentification, hallucination and prevarication.

Misidentification is clearly a cause of some Black Dog sightings just as ball lightning, Chinese lanterns and drones can generate mistaken UFO sightings. It is certainly possible that some of the witnesses saw a large black dog that, perhaps, behaved oddly.

The witness jumped to conclusions based on their local folklore or their desire to see something paranormal. If this slightly anomalous sighting also happened to be accompanied by a coincidental death in the family, some other disaster or storm, then the story would gain added mystery in the witness' mind.

What drives the narrative of Black Dog stories into the realm of the Otherworldly for me is that, while it is possible to explain some sightings as large sociable black dogs, the misidentification hypothesis would require a ready supply of immense black dogs sporting odd behaviours, scattered all over the UK, US, Canada and Latin America. Viewed in that light, the probability of misidentification over the whole of the Black Dog phenomenon drops precipitously.

When we add the high strangeness back into our sightings – glowing red eyes, vanishing as the witness watches, death rates post-sighting above statistical significance, attempts at physical interaction (petting or striking) that are unsuccessful, failure of bullets to affect the animal, standing on hind legs and more – we have a phenomenon that cannot consistently be shrugged off as misidentification.

I would also note that many of the witnesses in classic sightings from writers like Rudkin and Brown were country folk. As Theo Brown said, these people tend to be "the most sceptical of mortals" and, I would note, people who have a lot of familiarity with the local animals, including farm dogs and livestock. Again, it is always possible that a stray dog might cause a failure in identification, but it seems far more likely to me that the country person would look at a dog and think "By golly, old Shep from down the road has grown some" rather than assuming that the creature was supernatural.

The other two items in the skeptic's triad – hallucination and hoax – are more difficult to address, particularly in the context of Phantom Black Dogs.

Much of the folklore for the Black Dog comes from folklorists, people concerned with preserving a story and not getting a full witness statement from someone who has had a paranormal event. As such, many of our witness accounts are incomplete and entirely too short for us to draw any real conclusions, and other than the folklorist's note that the person they spoke to seemed to be of sound mind, we have no way of assessing whether this is true.

In looking at the idea that some witnesses might literally be seeing things, we do have some data. A recent Live Science article had the startling title "1 in 20 People Has Hallucinated" and went on to report that a study of 31,000 people in 18 countries reported that nearly 6% of respondents had experienced hallucination. The study screened out serious mental illness (like psychosis, for example) and drug or alcohol abuse.

This sounds like a lot of people, and it is, but a closer look at the article shows that the questions were about both hallucinations and delusions. Delusions are the false beliefs that some people have such as the thought that people are out to get them or that someone important is in love with them. Someone who is delusional might have a belief that Black Dogs are the result of secret government experiments, but they would not be seeing the dogs. The vision of a Black Dog to a person with a mental disorder would be a hallucination.

So, a hallucination and a delusion are two separate things; a delusion does not involve the "perception of something that is not physically present", as the dictionary definition goes. A more accurate title for the article would have been "1 in 20 People Have Had Hallucinations or Delusions". The article does not provide a breakdown of which people reported delusions, which reported hallucinations, and which reported both, so we do not have clear numbers.

A thorough reading of the article also makes the reader realize that the people doing the study screened out mental illness via self-reporting. In other words, if the respondent said that they had no history of mental illness, then that checked the box for "no mental illness present" for this study. Such self-reporting is not a reliable indicator of the presence or lack of mental illness, so, again, the numbers could be skewed by the presence of people with undiagnosed mental illness or those who lied about their diagnosis.

Given the hallucination/delusion dichotomy and the possibility that a number of undiagnosed or unreported mentally ill individuals could have been sampled, I would have to conclude that the number of people, of otherwise sound mind, with hallu-cinations is actually smaller than indicated in the banner headline.

Of course, hallucinations can also be brought on by physical illness, such as temporal lobe epilepsy, and by chemical means. It seems to me that, of all the strange things one might see in a hallucination, a large Black Dog with glowing red eyes is only one of an infinite variety of visions one could have.

The human mind has a nearly infinite store of images from which to choose, so, while I am prepared to admit that a few Black Dog stories could have been the result of mental disorder or picking the wrong mushrooms, I don't think that the number of stories generated by these causes comes anywhere close to explaining more than a tiny percentage of cases.

The final item in the skeptic's triad is, perhaps, the hardest to tackle. There are a certain percentage of people out there who will make a false report, and there are a variety of reasons why that "witness" might do that. I don't really want to get into the reasons why hoaxers hoax since those reasons can be opaque to outsiders.

In the end, it's very difficult to attach a number to any of these mundane reasons for Black Dog sightings. All we can say is that the skeptic's triad accounts for some percentage of witness reports, but it certainly does not account for all those reports or even, in my mind, the majority of the reports. As with the other paranormal creatures and objects that people see, human beings are encountering something on the highways and byways of their lands.

I think that we need to believe witnesses. Of course, we need to do everything we can to verify the stories that come to us. When we have the chance to go out into the field and investi-gate, we should certainly do so. In the case of the Black Dog and other apparitional accounts, we also need to look at the history and folklore of the place where the sighting occurred, any other stories or legends of the Black Dog in that area and, important to me, any tales from the indigenous peoples of the area.

I haven't run across any Black Dog stories in the lore of the aboriginal peoples, but it is certainly the case that there is a wide and varied history of Black Dog sightings throughout the areas we have discussed. Given that aboriginal people's accounts were often ignored, due to the prejudice against "primitives" and the tendency of tribal people to hold stories close to the chest until they know someone, I theorize that the First Nations people of the Americas probably have some stories about our subject that we haven't heard yet.

Now that we have had a chance to look at some of the mundane reasons for Black Dog reports, let's do a deeper dive and look at some of the more esoteric explanations for these incidents.

26

SPONTANEOUS PSYCHISM

BEFORE WE VENTURE into the deep end of the explanation pool for Phantom Black Dogs, let's look at an example of a phenomenon that has been scientifically proven, throughout many years, but that science has simply refused to accept: psychic phenomena. As do many researchers, I will refer to these phenomena as psi throughout this section.

Let's begin with an odd little tale from the path leading to Geldeston churchyard. The percipient is clearly having a psychic or clairvoyant vision, and M. H. James, the recorder of this account, notes that the witness was born in the "chime hours", that is between midnight and 0400, a time when people, according to the local culture of the sighting area, were allegedly born with special gifts, including the Sight, or clairvoyance.

> "Mrs. S", her daughter "A", and her daughter's young man Josh were walking one late evening on the "market path" back from Gillingham, and as they got over a stile onto Geldeston Road, "A" suddenly said "How that dog did frighten me!" The others saw nothing, but "A" said it was now walking slowly ahead of them. "Mrs. S" then heard a "thumping" sound, and "A" said

that were now "just agin it", at which Josh then struck about on the road with his stick, hitting nothing.

Then "Mrs. S" could see it when "A" took hold of her, but lost sight of it again every time she let go. They described it as a big black dog, or "like a black dog", but it "didn't keep the same size, and wasn't any regular shape." At one point, it was "bigger than a horse." Walking slowly so that it wouldn't get behind them, Josh then found that he too could hear the "thumping" sound. After about half a mile they passed a threeways known as the Gelders [TM39909190], where the dog then went on before them until it came to the sandy lane [TM39529196] leading to the churchyard, then "went off there." Very scared, "Mrs. S" and "A" went home, while Josh went back to Beccles.

"A" was born in the "Chime Hours", "so she could see things", while they found it terrible passing the Gelders, since "Mrs. S" "had seen things there before."

This is a classic example of a Black Dog sighting except for the visibility of the phenomenon. While some people in the group could hear certain sounds associated with the Black Dog, only A could see the animal unless she took hold of Mrs. S, who could see the Black Dog when A was touching her.

Interestingly, in *The Secret Commonwealth*, Robert Kirk describes a similar phenomenon. A seer, one who could see the faery subjects of Kirk's work, could grant temporary Sight to a person by being in contact with them, having the individual stand on one of the seer's feet and look over the seer's shoulder while gripping the seer's arm, for example. There were a number of signs that might indicate that one was born to be a faery seer, including being born at certain liminal times of the year, such as at the New Year, or being born with a caul, a part of the amniotic membrane, covering the face.

Such seers were both respected and feared since their interaction with the faery meant that one could provoke the "Little People" in provoking one of their seers. As I've noted before, provoking the fae is not the way to a calm and prosperous life.

In considering psychic abilities, a quote from Dr. Charles Tart, a researcher in the field of psychic phenomena, including the phenomenon of remote viewing (also known as travelling clairvoyance) will serve to get us started:

Scientism is a psychological process of taking the currently accepted scientific theories about how the universe functions and subtly starting to regard them as if they were the absolute truth, beyond any further serious questioning. A theory, always subject to further test and refinement, becomes a law. Thus the process of science becomes an "ism", becomes a psychological stopping point, becomes a dogmatic belief system, like many of our most dogmatic religions.

This is precisely the position that many, if not most, scientists take when it comes to so-called "fringe" topics. If you can simply wave your mental wand and proclaim that a topic is unscientific, then you have the power to dismiss anything that makes you uncomfortable. At that point, you have moved completely out of science and, as Dr. Tart notes, into the realm of a dogma that refuses to even consider the notion of things that it concludes are impossible. This viewpoint completely quashes a science based in the spirit of inquiry.

Chris Carter, in his excellent book *Science and Psychic Phenomenon*, explores this topic in great detail. Carter has also published works on science's relation to the near-death experience and the afterlife. All are worth a look to help the researcher understand what they are up against as they seek "proof" for their phenomenon.

Suffice to say that controlled, randomized, double-blind tests

– the gold standard of scientific research – have verified the existence of telepathy (mind to mind communication) and psychokinesis (physical effects with the mind) and that those tests have been successfully repeated, as required by the scientific method. The data for these subjects has shown itself to be statistically significant, time and again, and only the stubborn opposition of the followers of "scientism" has kept these phenomena from being accepted as worthy of study and, indeed, as workable hypotheses or even theories.

When we add to this research over a century of psychical research with its compilation of vast archives of anecdotal evidence in a variety of paranormal topics, we see just how strong this current of scientism has become. Despite the vast amount of evidence, both scientific and anecdotal, for the existence of psi, scientism has concluded that psychism is impossible and that, therefore, all persons investigating it are deluded.

Clairvoyance, the ability to perceive things beyond normal sensory contact or even in the future, has proven harder to test scientifically but has significant anecdotal support as well as government research which has been surprisingly confirmatory. The interesting results of experiments such as the Stargate program, which developed a method for bringing about psychic awareness and scored some amazing "hits" until the US government supposedly shut the program down, seem to point to the idea that we can regard clairvoyance as a working hypothesis that is still in the experimental process.

Remote viewing experiments and psi research have shown that the ability works best when the percipient is relaxed. Remote viewers, for example, go through what is called a cool down, a process whereby they induce relaxation and quiet their minds. The research has also shown that psi results fall off when percipients are placed under pressure to perform or simply become bored with the repetitive processes used for testing.

So, let's imagine for a moment our typical Black Dog encounter. A person has been walking or riding or driving for some period of time. It is near dusk or night has fallen so that sensory input is limited. We are not told specifically what is in most witnesses' mind at the time of the encounter, but we can, from our own experiences, extrapolate and hypothesize that the mind tends to wander during these activities.

In other words, the percipient has inadvertently wandered into an altered state of consciousness and has put themselves into the state of mind where they are most likely to receive psychic information. If you doubt that this could happen, I will point you to the well-documented phenomenon of meditation while walking that is popular in Zen Buddhism. I would also note that the Chinese Taoist traditions have numerous moving spiritual practices, such as Tai Chi Chuan and Chi Gung, that, once the movements are learned, will place one in a very quiet and receptive state of mind.

This concept of moving receptivity is demonstrated in a study by Tiffany Field and others that measured the effects of tai chi practice on various stress indicators including brain waves. The study showed, amongst other markers, an increase in theta brain waves amongst the tai chi participants. Theta brain waves are seen during sleep and deep meditation, but even if our imaginary percipient has only wandered down into the alpha brain state, their mind is still relaxed and receptive.

If our percipient has moved themselves into a calm state of mind, then psi is possible. I believe that at least some of our Black Dog encounters may be examples of spontaneous psychism that occurs as a result of walking, literally or figuratively, into this meditative or trance state. These witnesses literally wander into a vision of the Otherworld.

If the Black Dog is a psychic vision, this would explain the inability of some witnesses to touch the creature when they see it. Given the association of the Black Dog with death in the witnesses' family, an event that seems to occur more often than we could assume by chance, it is possible that the Black Dog is a clairvoyant vision, warning of the upcoming event.

Stories of clairvoyance in the face of death or disaster are common and often involve seeing dreams or daytime visions that may or may not make sense to the witness at the time. Mary Hyre, a reporter in the town of Point Pleasant, West Virginia, during the Mothman sightings, is said to have had a number of precognitive dreams before the collapse of the Silver Bridge.

In those dreams, she saw Christmas packages floating in the water. The dreams literally came true. Packages actually did float on the water when the suspension bridge collapsed and dozens of cars, containing Christmas shoppers, were dumped into the Ohio River.

My point in relating this example is that the world of psi has strong parallels with the world of dreams. Dreams operate on symbols. Might it not be true that the Black Dog can be a symbolic portent of death that manifests in spontaneous visions to certain people? It may even be that, as the Black Dog portent manifests to more and more people, it develops into an even stronger symbol.

I feel that this is entirely possible, and I think that some of our Black Dog sightings, particularly those that precede a death or disaster in a family, could be examples of spontaneous clairvoyance using the Black Dog as a symbol for the oncoming death.

We have to be cautious not to hang too much on this theory, however. We have examples of Black Dogs being seen during the day in conditions when the witness would have been alert – Coastguardsman Grant, for example – and we have instances of people seeing the Black Dog and taking actions that would not be conducive to the semi-trance needed for good psi performance. Remember that witnesses have tried to beat our Black Dogs with their fists, umbrellas and sticks as well as shooting at them. I suspect that such actions might exclude the psi hypothesis.

While spontaneous instances of psi may explain some of our cases, we need to go deeper into the woods of the unexplained for further theories.

27

GHOSTS?

IF YOU READ Mark Norman's book titled *Black Dog Folklore*, you will see Norman refer to Black Dogs as "ghost dogs" on a number of occasions. I object to this usage almost as firmly as I reject the styling of the Black Dog as a "hellhound".

Since about the fourteenth century, the term that became our modern English "ghost" was meant to refer to the discarnate remnants of a human being. Whether you call this spirit, soul or essence, the belief seems to be that some part of the human being survives death and may be capable of visiting those of us on this side of the Veil.

The Phantom Black Dog cannot be a ghost since it is obviously not human in form, nor does it behave in a human manner.

If we continue to follow this line of thinking, however, we note that there are those in the paranormal world who believe that animals, especially beloved pets, may also leave something behind after their deaths. By definition, we cannot call these remnants ghosts, so let's just refer to them as spirits.

I am prepared to harbour the belief in animal spirits, based on personal experience, but, again, the energetic remnants of such pets make their presence known in forms that their former human companions will recognize.

Here is an example. I spoke, in the introduction, of my own black dog, Echo. When Echo died, I had been working remotely for several years as my spouse travelled the US gaining job experience and then working on their PhD. Needless to say, Echo was my constant companion, and the jingling of her dog tags was a background noise I took for granted.

When my canine friend passed, my apartment was entirely too quiet. I would sit at my home office desk, working on the computer or involved in some teleconference call, and be conscious of just how quiet the place was without my black dog moving around in it.

One day, as I sat waiting for another meeting to start, I clearly heard Echo's tags jingling in the other room. The sound was so clear that I got out of my chair and went into the living room to look, almost believing that I would see Echo sitting there, giving me her usual quizzical look, her head cocked to the side and tongue lolling from her mouth.

She was not, of course, waiting for me, but I feel that she did pop by for a post-death visit. I had this experience on three separate occasions, along with occasional, corner-of-the-eye glimpses of a black "something" in a doorway, and it only stopped when I rescued another dog several months after Echo died. My sentimental side thinks that Echo figured I needed some company until another dog came into my life.

As with most witnesses, I will fight the skeptic who tells me that this experience was wishful thinking, but my story, and the stories of many other witnesses who have encountered their dead pets, points to a very real problem with the Black Dog being the spirit of a farm dog or other canine companion.

The people who have the experience of meeting their pet's "spirit" report that the experience is personal and that they have a very clear sense of a particular animal reaching out to them from across the Veil. The Black Dog, when it appears, does not meet these parameters at all.

I have never encountered a Black Dog story where the apparition was personal to the witness. In addition, it is plain that the Dogs in these stories often frighten the percipient. Animal spirits, returning to visit their human companions, do not typically bring fear but often, instead, seem to be messengers of hope, comfort or, at least, humour designed to pull their human out of mourning. I see none of these ideas present in the folklore of the Black Dog.

I note, too, that most of the stories that relate Black Dogs to ghosts tend to fall into the vengeful spirit category and are firmly housed in the realm of local legends and not witness accounts. Local legends often have a grain of truth in them, so I am loath to say that there are no Black Dogs that are vengeful spirits. I try to avoid absolutes in my thinking, and it is certainly the case that a massive, glowing-eyed Black Dog would make a good form for a spirit bent on vengeance. Such spirits, though, fall outside of the scope of this book, and I think there are far better explanations for the Black Dog.

While I am not a proponent of the Black Dog as ghost theory, both/and thinking requires that I look at all angles of this subject. One place where I think we might have an interface between Black Dogs and the world of ghosts is in the idea that some of these sightings might be explained by the spirits of extinct species.

In the Palm Spring sighting of Ron Palfrey in chapter 23, I noted that this is an area where the dire wolf once existed. *Canis dirus dirus* was a massive beast, slightly larger than the largest modern wolves, that lived ten to sixteen thousand years ago. While the insubstantiality of the Black Dog seems to argue against a relict population of these beasts, I see no reason why the occasional sighting might not actually be the spirit of a dark-coated specimen of one of these very large wolves.

Moving on to other, more deeply esoteric, subjects, from the Black Dog of Bungay to modern Black Dogs denoted as hell-hounds, the Black Dog has been associated in some human minds with what some call demons. I've already partially dealt with this topic in chapter 3, but I feel that we need to address the subject of demons/evil spirits before we pass on to two very interesting ideas from the world of magical practitioners.

28

DEMONS?

I AM DISTURBED by an increasing tendency in the paranormal world to label any slightly hostile paranormal entity as a demon. The terminology and the remedies for these supposed demonic incursions seem to derive solely from the Christian belief system and theology and ignore the fact that beings we might affirm as demons have been recognized by pre-Christian cultures all the way back to Babylon and Sumer.

While Christians comprise the largest single group of religionists in the world, there are, for example, an estimated one hundred million people who follow African Traditional Religions and who would look at the signs of a demonic incursion or even a possession in a completely different way. Those folks would also have an entirely different way of dealing with such spirits, if they chose to do so at all.

I think it behooves us to remember that the gods and spirits of one set of beliefs very easily become the demons of another. We see this, for example, in the Goetic spirit (normally referred to as a demon) Ashtaroth, whom many modern magicians would argue is simply a debased form of the Canaanite goddess Astarte (Ashtart).

It seems to me that the Phantom Black Dog gets labelled a demon simply because of the reaction that this being evokes in witnesses. In the section about the hellhound title, we spoke briefly about the demonization of that which humans fear.

While we do occasionally come across a witness who wants to pat the nice doggie that comes up beside them on the road, the majority of our witnesses say, along with the gentleman in chapter 23, that they hope "to never see such a creature again".

In truth, one of the most prevalent responses to the Black Dog that we see in the lore is terror. More than one hearty soul has tried to outrun our phantom or outrace it on a bicycle or even flee swiftly on a motorbike, to no avail.

If a being is this frightening, this terrifying, then it must certainly be evil, must it not?

Since those who like to fling around the "demon" word tend to be reliant on Christian definitions and that religion's scriptures for their evidence, I will cite an example of the fallacy of this argument from the Judeo-Christian tradition. If one argues that a being that terrifies people must be evil, then one must accept that angels are evil and should be shunted into the demon category, along with their reportedly fallen brethren.

Angels, in the Bible, are not the sweetness and light creatures that we hear about in modern recitations. They are supposed to be messengers of the Divine, and they are not to be trifled with. These beings are often depicted in bizarre ways, and, invariably, the first words they speak when encountering a human are some variant of the phrase "be not afraid". The immediate reaction of most people who see them is to fling themselves on their faces and beg for their lives.

If the Bible is to be believed – and that is entirely at the reader's discretion – an angel was responsible for the deaths of all the firstborn children in Egypt during the events leading to the Biblical exodus. This angel was so precise in carrying out its instructions that the Children of Israel had to mark their doors with lamb's blood to let the angel know to "pass over" them.

In addition, in 2 Kings, an angel stops Assyrian forces from invading Jerusalem by killing 185,000 men outside the city wall in one night. Angels, in Biblical and other folklore, are powerful beings with agendas that human beings often can't comprehend.

My point in bringing forth these examples is to note that the assignation of the moniker good or bad, demonic or angelic, is a difficult call for humans, with their limited perspective, to make.

If we demonize that which we fear, then there is an even deeper reason for our demonization of the Black Dog. As I noted in chapter 3, our subject is strongly associated with the aspect of existence that many humans fear most deeply: death.

Throughout the book, we have seen that while there is reason to believe that the Dog has been maligned on this score and that most witnesses meet with no ill fate, there are plenty of stories in which a sighting coincides with the death of the witness or a witnesses' family member. This seems to happen with a frequency that cannot be assigned to chance.

Does this fact make the Black Dog an evil creature or a demon?

This is only the case if we do not accept death as a natural part of life. As the saying goes, none of us are going to get out of here alive. There is nothing evil about death itself; one can look at it as simply the transition of life energy from one form to another or a recycling of that energy into the universal field or even a cessation of consciousness with who knows what happening next. The Black Dog and other death harbingers seem to me to be a reminder to live our lives fully every day so that, when our time does come, we can make our crossing without regrets.

We can take this a step further and look at the fact that the domestic dog has traditionally been seen as a psychopomp.

Ranging all the way from Anubis, through Cerberus and on to Garm, we see this theme repeat over and over. This line of thought is seen with the Aztecs and their belief, covered in the section on Latin America, that it was vitally necessary to have a dog help the newly deceased into the land of the dead. Given what we have learned of the Phantom Black Dog, I have no problem believing that the Black Dog might show up to help some recently deceased people make their transition to some other state or to guard those folks as they do so.

So, if frightening people does not make our phantom evil and its association with death does not make it evil, but may actually highlight its role as a psychopomp, then why do we see this persistent desire to label the Phantom Black Dog as a demonic entity?

As I mentioned in an earlier section of the book, some of the blame can be laid at the feet of modern journalism and entertainment. A lot can be said here, but, whether we are talking journalism or entertainment, content creators are looking for something that will grab the attention of the one reading or watching. One of the surest ways to focus a person is to offer them a scare, and thus the Phantom Black Dog, so beloved of writers like Rudkin and Brown, has become the slavering, lantern-eyed hellhound of modern media.

We can also lay the blame for the Black Dog's scary metamorphosis at the feet of the world's dominant religion.

The word "demon" derives from a Greek word "daimon" but a daimon was an entirely different thing from what we think of as a demon in this day and age. The daimon was simply a spirit, thought of as existing between the moon and the earth in Greek cosmology and thus referred to as sublunar.

These spirits were everywhere in the animistic worldview of our pre-Christian forebears. They inhabited all salient features of the land, and it was recognized that some daimon were willing to associate with human beings while others did not care for our race and were to be avoided.

Human beings worked with daimon and the more powerful spirits, which one might think of as gods or goddesses, as their religious practice before the coming of Christianity.

When the dualistic Christian creed began to spread across Europe, their Word said that those who were not with the Christian god were against the Christian god. This saying pertained to people, but it also pertained to spirits. The daimon, gods and goddesses with which pagan cultures had worked for centuries all fell into the category of demons, and Christian lore grew up to support the idea that these were angels that had fallen from grace and were bent on the condemnation of humans.

If we follow this line of reasoning, then it is easy to see how our sometimes frightening subject with its roots in the Underworld guardians Anubis, Cerberus and Garm was labelled demonic. Additionally, it's easy to forget the many stories of the Black Dog appearing to guard travellers and guide those lost in the fog. Remember the Latin American Cadejo that protected alcoholics so that it could harvest their souls when they died from their disease? Even the guardian Black Dog has been saddled with evil motives in that region.

Finally, I think that the Phantom Black Dog has been labelled a demon as a simple product of a failure in spiritual discernment. I do not deny the existence of demons, any more than I deny the existence of their counterparts, the angels. I would agree with Michelle Belanger's definition of a demon found in their *The Dictionary of Demons*:

> Generally speaking (and certainly of the purposes of this book), demons are agents of disaster and chaos that willfully visit suffering and disease upon mortals. They are not exclusive to Christianity, nor is the concept of demonic possession

exclusive to the Christian worldview. Demons are far older than Abrahamic religions, and many of our classic concepts of these antinomian beings have their roots in religious systems that were old before Christianity was even begun.

Belanger, in an online video, clarifies even further by noting that their criteria for calling a haunting entity a demon is very specific. The being must be nonhuman (in other words, not simply a nasty ghost), with a malevolent agenda aimed at living human beings. Additionally, the being must be self-aware and intelligent. It will be aware of the people it is victimizing and often seems to have a certain glee and harsh intent in its malice. Finally, Belanger states that a demon will have a certain intuitive feel that assists in discerning it from other spirits, ghosts, etc. I would add that the demon, as opposed to any other type of Otherworld entity, clearly seems to have an interest in obsessing and/or possessing human beings.

Personally, I think it is unfair to label Black Dogs as yet another evil spirit from the depths of Hell and, given the definition of a demon we have seen above, I don't think our apparition fits into this category at all. The Phantom Black Dog phenomenon is complex and varied and cannot be readily pigeonholed by an open-minded person. Many Sasquatch witnesses report absolute terror during their sighting, as do people who spot a UFO. Are we going to start saying that people saw a Hell Hominid or An Unidentified Flying Demon? Most Forteans would laugh at the suggestion and with good cause.

I think that our topic is quite spooky enough without adding demons into the mix and that there is no need to revert to the demonic to explain our subject, so let's move on to a couple of interesting magical theories that could support the Phantom Black Dog.

29

THE ENERGY MODEL: THOUGHT-FORMS

OUR NEXT POSSIBLE explanation for the Phantom Black Dog bears a close look, in my opinion, since it references a topic that many researchers are uncomfortable with: magic. In the continuing struggle for legitimacy, i.e., acceptance by the scientific establishment, many researchers are reluctant to look at the real and vibrant magical community still extant in the world today. No matter what we call these practitioners, they seem to have a core set of beliefs that we can look at to develop ideas about our topic.

For a justification of looking at "monsters" from a magical perspective, I, again, refer the reader to John Michael Greer's excellent *Monsters: An Investigator's Guide to Magical Beings*. I'll also be looking at the topic in this chapter from the point of view of a couple of ceremonial magicians as well as setting forth a theory of my own based on study of these two sources and others.

Energy is everywhere. The sun shines on a plant, and that plant uses photosynthesis to fuel its growth and other processes. You take energy in as the food you eat and, using a complex process of metabolism, use it to power the functions of your body.

On a more macro level, you plug a lamp into an outlet, and electrical energy turns that light on. If you have been in a traffic accident, a doctor might use various forms of energy to image the inside of your body to get an idea of where you are or aren't broken. Kirlian photography records an energy signature around the human body and even plants that some people claim is the aura that psychics and mystics see.

Those who follow the energy model of magical practice see human beings as swimming in an ocean of energy. Some magical practitioners take this whole idea of energy a step (or a giant leap) further. They actually believe that intention, visualization and desire are also energies and can be used to effect physical reality.

In magical practices of varying kinds, including the widely overused example of Tibetan tulpas, we find a particular kind of magical construct that has a direct bearing on our subject. These constructs have been called by various names, but, to stick closely to the Western occult tradition with which I am most familiar, I will refer to these magical constructs as thought-forms.

In her novel *The Secrets of Doctor Taverner*, the occultist Dion Fortune (real name: Violet Firth) has a story that opens with the narrator, Dr. Rhodes, concluding his examination of a man. The good doctor concludes that the patient has a weak heart and that too much exertion could kill him. Rhodes' colleague, John Taverner, takes over as the man is complaining that his mind is giving him shocks that could kill him.

The patient tells a horrifying tale of a mastiff-like black dog that appears from nowhere to frighten him. The creature will appear at his side while he is out walking or make its presence known in the patient's rooms, then close on the man when he becomes aware of it. As the beast comes nearer, the patient seeks to banish the dog by repeating to it that it is not real. The beleaguered man has so far resisted the temptation to flee from his harasser, but he is not certain how much longer he can hold out.

Dr. Taverner derives a clue about where this apparition is coming from when the patient notes that the dog does not appear on Friday nights. As this is the night that the local "Black Lodge" meets, Taverner becomes aware that this may be a case of attempted magical murder. As he puts it:

> This is a clear case of mental assassination. Someone who is a trained occultist has created a thought-form of a black hound, and he is sufficiently in touch with Martin [the victim in this case] to be able to convey it to his mind by means of thought transference, and Martin sees, or thinks he sees, the image that the other man is visualizing.

Of course, the good doctor is able to resolve the case by tracking down the occultist who is harassing his patient and returning the thought-form to its maker with drastic results for that unfortunate man. There are a number of interesting, fictionalized cases in this work that will give the explorer of high strangeness new avenues of exploration, if he or she dares.

Now, while this is a fictional account, Fortune was a well-known occultist who published many non-fiction esoteric books. The legend in occult circles, given Fortune's own interest in psychiatry, was that the accounts in the book are based on actual cases she worked with her mentor.

This idea is fortified by her presentation of an interesting thought-form story in her book *Psychic Self-Defence*, a non-fiction work. Fortune is commenting on an accident she had while she was still a novice in esoteric matters. The following story is an example of how thoughts can, if properly focused, turn into the potential for a psychic attack in a form we might recognize:

> I had received serious injury from someone who, at considerable cost to myself, I had disinterestedly helped, and I was sorely tempted to retaliate. Lying on my bed resting one afternoon, I was brooding over my resentment, and while so brooding, drifted towards the borders of sleep. There came to my mind the thought of casting off all restraint and going berserk. The ancient Nordic myths rose before me, and I thought of Fenris, the Wolf-horror of the North. Immediately I felt a curious drawing out sensation from my solar plexus, and then materialised beside me on the bed a large wolf. It was a well-materialised ectoplasmic form. Like Z., it was grey and colourless, and like him, it had weight. I could distinctly feel its back pressing against me as it lay beside me on the bed as a large dog might ...

Z was Fortune's mentor, and, in a previous account, she related how he had appeared to her during a time when he was ill. The apparition had actually had a physical presence to her, sitting beside her on her bed. Fortune goes on to tell the reader that she went immediately to her teacher but, even with his instruction, had a devil of a time retrieving and neutralizing the thought-form she had created.

Now, I would note that this incident happened before Fortune became the formidable occultist that she was later reputed to be. While she had, at this point, had some training in magical techniques, this apparition was more a result of her natural talent than any magic she was working.

What if someone with experience in magical matters wants to create a thought-form? I can think of no better reference for this process than the work of Dolores Ashcroft-Nowicki, who once served as Director of Studies for Servants of the Light (SOL), a magical order that derives from Dion Fortune's Society of the Inner Light.

Ashcroft-Nowicki, along with SOL initiate J. H. Brennan, wrote *Magical Use of Thought Forms*, a fascinating book and one which all those interested in these subjects might want to read. In particular, the first section of the book covers many incidences of high strangeness that the authors relate to the use of thought-forms.

According to Ashcroft-Nowicki, a thought-form is brought about by the Triangle of Causation: desire, visualization and imagination. Desire is defined as a "single-mindedness of will". Visualization is the ability to "create or recreate images in the mind's eye and retain them ..." Imagination allows one to "create a scenario using symbols, locations, events, and effect, weaving them around the desired object". The process of imagination is one that authors use when creating novels, and Ashcroft-Nowicki advises studying novels as a way of developing this faculty.

Of course, there is quite a lot more to learning the skill of consciously creating a thought-form, but, given the experience of Fortune above, it may be possible that these "well-materialised ectoplasmic form[s]" are sometimes created quite by accident. It is also true that those skilled in the use of creating these images create them for their own purposes.

I don't think that it is a coincidence that one of the foremost occultists of the twentieth century wrote a story in which a member of a "Black Lodge" sought to slay someone with an image that was modelled on the Black Dog. Given Fortune's Fenris incident and then adding the interesting stories linked to thought-forms by J. H. Brennan in the *Magical Use of Thought Forms*, we see that the creation of these "beings", either accidentally or deliberately, could account for some of the stories included in this book.

Thought-forms may be created to serve any purpose the creator desires (single-mindedness). It may be that some of our Black Dogs were set into place to guard an area, to achieve some task that we are unaware of, to put a scare into a rival or, perhaps, to chase some poor bastard over a cliff. While the process of creating a thought-form is not simple or easy, there have certainly been people, throughout history, who are capable of this act.

While I view this type of magic as very possible, I don't think that the conscious creation of thought-forms happens frequently. It is, as I say, a lot of work and requires intense training. I would think that there are easier ways to achieve one's desires.

My personal theory in this regard is that it is far more likely that a thought-form might be created by a mass of people, all focused on the same or a very similar idea.

Forteans have long puzzled over the appearance of the Slenderman, a being that originated as a character in internet fiction and then seemingly took on a life of its own. Slenderman was a character that was formulated in fans' minds, then drawn and obsessed over by dozens if not hundreds of people. These people then began to write stories assigning motive and character to the monster.

If we look at the information from *Magical Use of Thought Forms*, we see that we have the elements of the triad used to create a thought-form. Single-mindedness, visualization, and imagination and, as a bonus, a whole lot of emotional energy as fans worked harder and harder to scare themselves and each other with this new monster. I think it highly possible that the people on the *creepypasta* fiction site either created the monster out of whole cloth or created a form for some existing spirit to assume.

In like manner, legends of the Phantom Black Dog go back for centuries, the people who are aware of those legends have a distinct visual image of the creature, and there are stories told of the Black Dog all throughout the lands where it makes its home.

Might not some of the apparitions people are seeing be thought-forms created by this folkloric process? Or perhaps the Phantom Black Dog is exactly what it seems to be, an incursion from some Otherworld.

30

SPIRIT MODEL: ANIMISM

IF WE THINK of magic as a "way of thinking that looks to invisible forces to influence events, effect change in material conditions, or present the illusion of change" (from the Britannica encyclopedia), then there must be a mechanism that makes magic possible. We've already explored one of those great models, the energy model.

The other explanation for the efficacy of magic is the spirit model.

Before there was any such thing as scientific materialism, humans operated on another paradigm completely, the animist paradigm. I gave a detailed definition of animism in the introduction to this section of the book, but briefly, animism posits that all things in our seemingly physical world have an essence that we might even call a spirit. Please see Tobias Wayland's wonderful quote at the beginning of this section for a glimpse of how an animist might see the world.

There was a time when this worldview was quite common and what the Greeks called daimon inhabited every nook and cranny in nature. I believe we see this idea in belief systems ranging from the manitou of the indigenous people of the area where I now live to the faery beliefs of the Celtic countries to the belief, found in the seventy-second chapter of the Quran, in the djinn of the Islamic world.

All over the earth, in indigenous, folk and neopagan beliefs, there are spirits that inhabit the natural world, beings that we cannot see, and which can be beneficial to humans, indifferent to them or downright hostile. These discarnate entities seem to also include at least some of the human dead, thus the seeming confusion in faery lore between the dead and the fae.

In faery lore, the fae live underground or within the Land. This place "under hill" is recognized as another world altogether, with rules all its own. We learn, by reading this lore, that the fae can pass from their world into ours, and while they are in our world, they can be seen and have a physical effect on their environment.

Famously, the faery species known as a brownie is known for its housecleaning acumen, and there are even reports of faery blood in human bloodlines, which imply a physical relationship between a human and one of these beings. Books like Evan-Wentz's *The Fairy Faith in Celtic Countries* and Janet Bord's *Fairies: Real Encounters with the Little People* document sightings of these beings and the measures that folk took, a little over a hundred years ago, to maintain good relations with them.

Robert Lebling, in his expansive work on the djinn, *Legends of the Fire Spirits*, tells us that the djinn live amongst humankind but that we cannot normally see them. It is accepted in Islamic culture that the beings are there but exist in a slightly different dimension from our own, one from which they can pass and thus enter our world at will. Interestingly, the djinn are seen as shape-shifters, and one of their favorite forms, when they are on this side of the Veil, is a black dog. Those dogs are seen as solid and real when they are in our plane of reality.

Traditional indigenous people throughout the Americas and in the Pacific Islands take it for granted that there are spirits, which they call by various names, who walk among us when they will, crossing back and forth between the Otherworld and our own with facile ease. Linda Godfrey, in her book *Monsters Among Us,* mentions the Ho Chunk people of her region. Members of this tribe have told the author that Sasquatch is a spirit that lives in the Otherworld but can step through to our world and take on physical form.

From the Night Marchers of the Hawaiian Islands to the faery rades reported in Celtic faery lore, we learn that these beings are among us, can be seen when they enter our world, and seem to often be on the move. Many of these spirits appear to have the ability to affect their physical surroundings if they so desire or remain ethereal. Additionally, these sources tell us that the dead intermingle with and may account for some of these beings.

The question that I would pose is why? Why would different cultures all across the globe hold this belief? What is it in their experience, right up to the modern day, that makes them hold these beliefs? Why not simply throw up their hands, admit that science was right all along, and that the world is simply dead matter governed by a set of clockwork rules? Why cling to a belief that there are Others, as I like to call them, among us, as close to us as our own breath?

I would say simply that it is because their experience tells them that this is intuitively true.

Now, you, my reader, may choose to believe whatever you wish but please indulge me in a little thought experiment. Let's say, just for a moment, that all the people I have listed above are correct and that there is an Otherworld, populated by a vast array of Others, and that some of those beings can cross into our world. These beings may not be completely corporeal, but sometimes we can see them when they come through, and sometimes, perhaps, we can even touch them.

If we look at Fortune's idea of an ectoplasmic materialization, then we even have a situation where the Others can take on physical form. I knew a group of witches who believed that the Others could take on form by gathering material from the etheric realm, the plane of existence that touches our own. Whether we are talking ectoplasm or etheric substance, something that Greer also talks about in his book, magic provides us with a mechanism for the Others to appear in our world and for them to have substance, at least for a time.

It also provides some methods of dissolving those manifestations, for example, the use of the cold iron so dreaded by the faery, or the First Nations' use of sage in smudging. I learned from the group I mentioned above that iron will disrupt an etheric manifestation and that sage helps prevent entities from gathering the etheric substance, whatever you wish to call that.

Suddenly, we have a quite reasonable explanation for our Phantom Black Dog. Clearly, the Black Dog is an apparition, that is, something that appears to our senses, but the question then becomes, where is the apparition coming from? If we accept, along with people all over the world, that there are Others and that those beings, for purposes of their own, cross over from their world into ours, then we can place the Phantom Black Dog squarely into their realm.

If we are indeed surrounded by a vast ecosystem of discarnate beings and those beings can make themselves known to us, then it makes sense to me that some of them might appear to us as very large, black dogs with glowing eyes (amongst other things).

Short of sitting a Phantom Black Dog or some other apparition down for a chat, an unlikely notion since these beings are seldom known to speak or even communicate telepathically, we cannot know for certain where they come from, how they get into our world, and where they go when they vanish. All we can say for certain is that the spirit model, working out of magical thought, does have a certain inner consistency when viewed against the lore of the Phantom Black Dog.

There is one final theory that I want to take a look at. In the next chapter, we will encounter another esoteric theory that provides us with even more ideas about how our apparition might manifest.

31

LEY LINES

ONE OF THE common denominators of Black Dog lore is the prevalence of roadside sightings amongst the witness accounts. We see this, as well, in the percipients of other types of high strangeness events. Everything from Sasquatch to Dogmen to the Lizard Man of Scape Ore swamp seems likely to scare the bejesus out of someone as the witness is driving along a road or even fixing a flat tire, often late at night.

Recently, while looking at some old UFO cases, I was reminded that Betty and Barney Hill began their life-changing encounter while traveling a highway. Lonnie Zamora was on patrol for the Socorro police in New Mexico, driving a road, when his account begins. Even my own father claimed to have a UFO encounter while driving on a highway outside San Bernardino, California, in the 1950s, well before my birth.

The Phantom Black Dog takes this obsession with roads a step farther. While you might expect a dog-like entity from the Otherworld to run wild on the moors of England, the lore shows that you are far more likely to run into our subject on a roadside, coming out of a hedge. All through the research for this book, I have asked myself why these apparitions are so attracted to roads, and the inestimable Janet and Colin Bord propose a solution in their classic *Alien Animals*.

In the United Kingdom, certain researchers of the earth mysteries have developed a theory about earth energies. They started with certain Neolithic sites in the UK, places like Stonehenge, Avebury, and Glastonbury Tor. Looking at these sites on a map, it became clear to some of the researchers that these sites could be connected by straight lines and, furthermore, that some of those lines actually existed in the form of ancient straight tracks or roads! The name given to these straight tracks was ley lines.

Given the powerful energy that some sensitives sense at the ancient places, the theory is that these ley lines represent channels through which the energy of the earth travels somewhat like the meridians that channel the body's internal energy in traditional Chinese medicine.

The Bords are proponents of this theory and cite another of their works, *The Secret Country*, for those who want more information on the hypothesis. Honestly, after looking at their work on these tracks, relating to the Phantom Black Dog, I think one might need more mathematical savvy than I have to plot ley lines.

What is important to our discourse is that the Bords ran a preliminary survey of Black Dog sites in Lincolnshire, the home territory of researcher Ethel Rudkin, and found that several of the sites she mentions in her seminal article fall on ley lines. They obligingly gave the reference points for those leys in *Alien Animals* for other researchers to follow up on.

Why is this important?

I could refer back to faery lore again, but, to give the reader a break from one of my other obsessions, let's consider the work of John Keel. In *The Mothman Prophecies* and other of his works, Keel posits something that he calls a "window area", a place like

Point Pleasant, West Virginia, where high strangeness seems to occur in abundance. While Keel does not use these words exactly, shamans, witches, magicians (such as Dion Fortune, for example) and spiritualists might refer to these window areas as places where the Veil Between the Worlds is thin. Language would depend on what culture we are talking about, but the idea is the same.

Keel doesn't really address what causes these window areas; I think he may have been too busy watching UFOs sail down the Ohio River and hunting Mothman through the TNT area to be concerned with the how of what he was seeing. He throws out a lot of background information about his area of interest, starting with a supposed Indian curse and moving forward, but does not seem to lay the blame for the bizarre occurrences in Point Pleasant anywhere.

If we look at the theory of ley lines, however, we might have an answer. West Virginia, by itself, has something like 424 "Indian mounds", ancient locations that served as burial and sacred sites. Like Stonehenge and other Neolithic sites in the UK, these locations could be considered holy places.

Ohio, across the river, has an additional eighty sites. As I've said, I don't have the necessary geomantic chops to draw this out, but I would conjecture that, if some motivated and math-minded researcher took the time to map ley lines in that area, one or more of the straight lines would pass through or near Point Pleasant, and there might even be an intersection of lines in or near the town.

Returning to our Black Dogs, if we are talking about a creature of the Otherworld that moves into our world on a regular basis, would it not make sense that the entity uses the path of least resistance to get here, i.e., a ley line full of geomagnetic energy where the Veil is already likely to be thin?

Additionally, magical sources agree with modern physics.

Energetically, there are no free rides. If energy is required to accomplish tasks on our plane, then an energy exchange is necessary to make the transition from the Otherworld into this world and back. It seems to me that it would be easier for our Black Dogs to move between worlds using the energy of the ley line rather than trying to brute force the entrance themselves, if they are even able to do so.

While there are other ways that the Veil Between the Worlds might be weakened (see the conclusion of this text for some ideas), it certainly seems to me that the use of ley lines and areas filled with the Earth's geomagnetic energy would ease the transition for the Others. Authors such as Linda Godfrey and Nick Redfern have noted the prevalence of high strangeness in the regions around sacred sites of all sorts.

Sacred sites, in the ley theory, are often found at the juncture of two or more straight tracks. It makes sense that the Others would take advantage of the "free" energy at these sites to make their transition and manifestation easier.

We have covered a wide swathe of ground over the previous pages. We've defined the subject of our interest, laid out some ideas about where the Phantom Black Dog might be found, outlined some interesting aspects of high strangeness that accompany these cases, and presented some theories, ranging from mundane to worldview distorting, about the Black Dog. Let's conclude with some final thoughts on our glowing-eyed canids.

CONCLUSION

How often have I said to you that when you have
eliminated the impossible, whatever remains,
however improbable, must be the truth?

Arthur Conan Doyle
From "The Sign of Four"

As we have seen, the Phantom Black Dog is not a subject that
can be easily categorized. While the apparition has been seen
historically and in the present time both in the United States
and in Latin America as well as in the United Kingdom and
Ireland, most of the data collection for the phenomenon has
been folkloric in nature. That is, the researcher was trying to be
certain that the stories were collected and that was all.

As I've noted throughout this text, that approach has given
us a richness of really interesting stories, but it has often left us
painfully frustrated as well. Sometimes, the collected stories will

be one or two lines, and we will be left with an incredible witness statement and no details.

I picture a folklorist walking up to a farmer at the market and asking if they have heard anything about Phantom Black Dogs and the old fellow saying, "Sure! Saw the danged thing over on the market road a couple of months ago. It came out of the hedges, right about dusk, and walked along beside my wagon. Then my horse spooked, and I had to pay attention to driving so I didn't lose my load. Looked back, and the danged thing was gone. Weird eyes, I tell you!"

The folklorist might ask the witness' name and a couple of clarifying questions, but that is about all the story we get. Can you imagine sitting this farmer down and having a real interview with him? I certainly can.

It seems, when we research this topic, that the well-told, detailed stories are often the legends of the Black Dog and not the actual witness statements. We're never going to "solve" the mystery of this phantom because it is a phantom, and even if, as I suggested in the previous section, we adopt a more animistic view of the phenomenon, we still find ourselves on uncertain ground since modern-day science does not have equipment for assessing beings from the Otherworld.

As Colm Kelleher and George Knapp note in their book *Hunt for the Skinwalker*, about the mysteries surrounding the so-called Skinwalker Ranch, the phenomena do not simply present themselves over and over, repeating for the benefit of scientists trying to monitor them. This is true of both the phenomena at the notorious ranch and the Phantom Black Dog.

If we try to look at the Phantom Black Dog with the jaded eyes of modern-day scientism, we will be reduced to seeing the Dog as a case of mistaken identity, a hallucination or a hoax. I have not denied in these pages that such explanations could account for some of the Black Dog sightings on the books, but the lore is far too rich for us to dismiss all accounts in this way.

As Colm Kelleher and the National Institute of Discovery Science (NIDS) team discovered when they attempted to document the mysteries of that remote ranch in Utah, they, the scientists, were not in control. The team, after numerous paranormal encounters and sightings on the property, actually came to the conclusion that not only were they faced off with phenomena they could not explain but that whatever was directing the phenomena was intelligent and perhaps even precognitive.

The one thing that they were all agreed upon was that the phenomena refused to repeat itself, so what had begun as an intensive effort to study and document unidentified aerial phenomena was quickly turned into a wide-ranging game of hide-and-seek. Ordinary scientific method simply does not work with encounters and sightings that refuse to repeat themselves at convenient times and locations and that work to actively sabotage the measurement instruments.

Interestingly, odd canines played a role in the Skinwalker saga. The first recorded sighting in the book had the "Gorman" (a pseudonym used to protect the family at that time) family encountering what appeared to be a giant wolf, which strolled up to the humans in a friendly manner before seizing and trying to drag off a calf.

Mr. Gorman opened fire on the animal with a .357 Magnum pistol and later a hunting rifle. The bullets appeared to have no effect whatsoever, and the creature loped away from the scene. The giant wolf was then tracked to a creek bed, where its tracks abruptly disappeared.

Given the number of times we have seen the Phantom Black Dog vanish in this text, we can have some sympathy for the family's bewilderment.

The part of this story that really interested me was that,

some time later, Mrs. Gorman was returning to the ranch from her local job and saw this enormous wolf, or one similar to it, at very close range. Kelleher and Knapp reported that: "... easily visible in the gathering twilight was another animal, all black. It stood farther away from the car and appeared more reserved. It was large but not quite as large as the wolf. It looked like a very weird dog but unlike any she had ever seen".

The wolf in question was estimated at four times the size of a normal wolf, so this Black Dog would have been quite a whopper, too!

Later, after a series of bizarre events and the arrival of NIDS, Mr. Gorman went out with NIDS investigators to check on cattle in the fields and encountered two giant creatures, one a panther-like being with glowing yellow eyes that was up in a tree and the second a "huge, heavily muscled" four-hundred-pound wild dog of an unknown sort.

There is no mention of the animal being black, but, once again, gunfire from the rancher was shrugged off, and the animals went on their way. I would note here that we have seen several witness statements where the Black Dog is described as large and heavily muscled, so our phantom could have been making a guest appearance at the notorious ranch.

We've seen throughout this book that the Phantom Black Dog can take a number of forms, ranging from the spaniel-like Black Dog of the Hanging Hills, to the more massive dogs reported on both sides of the Atlantic. We've seen the Dog shrug off blows with hands, canes and umbrellas and sometimes walk on its hind legs. We have even heard stories of the Dog changing size and even shape, including taking on human form.

Even the Black Dog's personality is malleable. In a good many stories, we see our hound guarding travellers as they make their way home, but we also see Black Dogs like the one that visited Bungay in 1544 and allegedly caused so much chaos and death. Black Dogs can seem aggressive, friendly, or indifferent to the witness, depending on concerns we can only guess at.

As NIDS noted at Skinwalker Ranch, about the only thing consistent about the Phantom Black Dog is its inconsistency. Until, that is, we begin to look at the locations where the Dog is seen.

As I have repeated a number of times in these pages, the Black Dog is most often seen trotting beside a road or crossing a road. A road is, by definition, a liminal area, that is a place that occupies a position at or on both sides of a boundary or threshold. Also, consider the number of Black Dogs that appear at boundaries between two counties, districts, or parishes in the UK.

A liminal area is what faery lore might call betwixt and between, a place that is neither here nor there, and a road, since its purpose is to take us from here to there, falls firmly into the liminal spaces.

So too do a number of sightings occur near water. A beach or the bank of a creek is on the border between earth and water, as is that quintessential borderland, a marsh or swamp. Bridges that cross over water are in between one bank and the other.

The association of the Black Dog with churchyards, cemeteries and historical sites starts to make sense when looked at through the lens of liminality. All of these places are sites where the ultimate liminality is evident; they are sites at the border between the land of the living and the land of the dead.

Looking at the stories of Black Dogs in homes, we do not necessarily have to give up our theory that the Black Dog is walking the borderlands. Houses are usually found on roads, thus they are at least close to a liminal site already, but if we take out our rulers and maps and begin plotting ley lines, it is easily possible that these residences sit on one of the old straight tracks, another and more energetic example of liminality.

In faery lore, a home that sat on one of the ways that the faery trod in their wanderings was liable to experience ill luck unless the homeowners provided a way for the beings of the Otherworld to travel through, such as opening the windows and doors at night.

I think, too, that we have to consider the possibility that we humans are creating thin spots in the Veil Between the Worlds by our own actions. Think for a moment about the aboriginal tie-in for many areas of high strangeness:

- Point Pleasant has its curse of Chief Cornflower that is one of the earliest history pieces John Keel hands us when discussing the Mothman and other assorted weirdness in that West Virginia town.
- The Bridgewater Triangle area has Hockomock Swamp, a name that translates as something like "place of the spirits", and there is an intense history of conflict between the First Nations people of the region and European settlers.
- Linda Godfrey mentions repeatedly the correlation between Manwolf sightings and areas sacred to local or historical tribes.
- The late J. C. Johnson of Crypto Four Corners reported on and investigated a wide array of strangeness in the Four Corners area of the US, a region that sits firmly on tribal land.
- Skinwalker Ranch has the obvious tie-in with the path of the Skinwalker legend of the Ute people of that area.

All of the tribal people in these regions held some version of animistic beliefs, and all had spiritual practitioners who worked between the worlds, what some call shaman or medicine people. Might it not be possible that repeated interaction with the Otherworld in a particular area thins the Veil and allows beings from that world to more easily visit us?

If we take that idea a step further, a quick trip to the local bookstore can be an eye-opening experience. I guarantee you that I can walk into any well-stocked big-box bookstore right now and find copies of books on magic and shamanism that provide instructions on various ways to interact with the Otherworld. I further guarantee you that there are people, on any given day, who are working actively with these concepts and doing their best to visit the Otherworld and interact with its residents or to call the Other onto our side of the Veil.

No one has taken an accurate census of magical and shamanic practitioners, either in the US or Canada, but a 2001 American Religious Identification Survey identified 134,000 Wiccans, a neopagan group that often practices magic in the United States. Estimates of the number of American Wiccans range as high as one million at present, but it is very difficult to get an accurate number of these practitioners since many neopagans are not open about their religious practices.

If we add in all the people who are members of esoteric orders and other magico-religious organizations as well as practitioners of modern neo-shamanism, we have the biggest boom in people who want to walk between the worlds that our ordinary reality has likely ever seen. Is it any wonder that we are seeing reports of all manner of high strangeness if we have people working to thin the Veil every day?

Before the reader thinks that I am opposed to all this activity, I am not. I see it as a perfectly normal and healthy reaction from a part of the populace that is craving a direct experience of spirit outside the carefully controlled teachings and restrictions of religion.

Our Black Dog, despite its changeableness, is constant in

this one thing. It is a walker of the borderland areas, the places betwixt and between. Perhaps these are the places where it finds it easiest to make its transition from one world to the next, for purposes of its own. Perhaps, like a human who fancies a walk on the beach, the borderland areas are simply its preferred spot for an evening stroll. Perhaps, the Phantom Black Dog is, in some way, a guardian of these borderland areas, intended to keep unwary humans from wandering into places from which they might not return.

Regardless of the reason why the Phantom Black Dog chooses the borderlands, it seems that this apparition, which has haunted history and continues to haunt the present day, is here to stay. As we have seen, the apparition may evolve in some ways, but I believe that it will continue to be easily identifiable as the enormous, black dog with glowing saucer-sized eyes that stalks the highways and byways of the world, appearing suddenly and disappearing just as quickly, leaving puzzled, frightened witnesses in its wake.

BIBLIOGRAPHY

Folklore Articles and Books

Barber, P. (1988). *Vampires, burial, and death: Folklore and reality*. Yale University Press.

Barrett, W. H., & Garrod, R. P. (1976). *East Anglian Folklore and Other Tales*. Routledge & Kegan Paul Books.

Blundell, N. & Boar, R. (1983) "The Worlds' Greatest Ghosts". *Octopus*.

Briggs, Katharine. (2003). *A Dictionary of British Folk-Tales in the English Language*. Routledge.

Brown, A. (2002). *Haunted Places in the American South*. Univ. Press of Mississippi.

Brown, T. (1958). The Black Dog. *Folklore*, /69/(3), 175-192.

Brown, T. (1982). *Devon Ghosts*. Norwich: Jarrold & Sons Ltd.

Bunn, I. (1977). Black Shuck, Parts 1, 2 and 3. *Lantern (newsletter) 18, 19 & 20*.

Burchell, S. (2007). *Phantom Black Dogs in Latin America*. Heart of Albion Press. (Author's note: this book can be found in PDF form on the publisher's website at https://www.hoap.co.uk/pbdla.pdf)

Carr, K. (2018). *Hellhounds and Helpful Ghost Dogs: Conflicting*

Perceptions of "Man's Best Friend" Encoded in Supernatural Narrative. All Graduate Plan B and other Reports. 1337.

Dahlgren, M. V. (1882). *South-Mountain Magic: A Narrative*. McClain Printing Company.

Evans-Wentz, W. Y. (2003). *The Fairy Faith in Celtic Countries: The Classic Study of Leprechauns, Pixies, and Other Fairy Spirits*. Citadel Press.

Fleming, A. (1820). *A Straunge and Terrible Wunder: Wrought Very Late in the Parish Church of Bongay*. Reprinted for T. and H. Rodd.

Fraser, M. L. (1932). *Folklore of Nova Scotia*. Catholic Truth Society of Canada.

Green, C. & McCreery, C. (1975). *Apparitions*. Hamish Hamilton.

James, M.H. (1891). *Bogie Tales of East Anglia*. Pawsey & Hayes.

Kirk, R. (1976). *The Secret Commonwealth*. Brewer for Folklore Society.

*(Author's note: there is an excellent edition of this work published under the title *Walker Between the Worlds* edited with extensive commentary by the noted occultist R. J. Stewart)

MacGregor, A.A. (1955). *The Ghost Book*. Robert Hale.

MacManus, D. A. (1973). *The Middle Kingdom: The Faerie World of Ireland*. Colin Smythe Limited.

Marlowe, C. (1927). *People and Places in Marshland*. Palmer.

Norman, Mark. (2015). *Black Dog Folklore*. London: Troy Books.

Porter, Enid. (1974). "Fairies, Ghosts, and Black Dogs." In *The Folklore of East Anglia*. 89–92. Totowa, NJ: Rowman and Littlefield.

Randolph, V. (1964). *Ozark Magic and Folklore*. Courier Corporation.

Reeve, C. (1988) *A Straunge and Terrible Wunder*. Morrow.

Rudkin, E. H. (1938). The black dog. *Folklore*. /49/(2), 111–131.

Sherwood, S. J. (2006) "Black Dogs of England", *Australian Folklore*. 21, pp. 16–29.

Stone, Alby. (1994). Hellhounds, Werewolves and the Germanic Underworld. *Mercian Mysteries*. /20/.

Tongue, R. L. (1956). *Traces of Fairy Hounds in Somerset*. Folklore. /67/(4), 233–234.

Tongue, R. L. (1970). *Forgotten Folk-Tales of the English Counties*. Routledge & Kegan Paul.

White, Thomas. (2010). *Ghosts of Southwest Pennsylvania (Haunted America)*. The History Press.

Wilder, Annie. (2012). *Trucker Ghost Stories: And Other True Tales of Haunted Highways, Weird Encounters and Legends of the Road*. Tor Books.

Witcutt, W. P. (1942). The Black Dog. *Folklore*. /53/(3), 167–168.

Woods, B. A. (1954). The Devil in Dog Form. *Western Folklore*. /13/(4), 229–235.

Zmarzlinski, A. (2020). The Black Dog: Origins and Symbolic Characteristics of the Spectral Canine. *Cultural Analysis*. /18/(2).

Fortean Titles

Blackburn, L. (2013). *Lizard Man: The True Story of the Bishopville Monster*. Anomalist Books.

Bord, J., & Bord, C. (1980). *Alien Animals*. Stackpole Books.

Bord, J. (1997). *Fairies: Real Encounters with the Little People*. Michael O'Mara Books Limited.

Clelland, M. (2015). *The Messengers*. Richard Dolan Press.

Cutchin, J. (2016). *The Brimstone Deceit: An In-Depth Examina-*

tion of Supernatural Scents, Otherworldly Odors, and Monstrous Miasmas. Anomalist Books.

Cutchin, J. & Renner, T. (2020). *Where the Footprints End: High Strangeness and the Bigfoot Phenomenon, Volumes I and II.* Independently Published.

Godfrey, L. S. (2011). *Monsters of Wisconsin: Mysterious Creatures in the Badger State.* Stackpole Books.

Godfrey, L. S. (2012). *Real Wolfmen: True Encounters in Modern America.* Tarcher/Perigree.

Godfrey, L. S. (2015). *The Beast of Bray Road: Trailing Wisconsin's Werewolf.* Dystel & Goderich Literary Management.

Godfrey, L. S. (2020). *I Know What I Saw: Modern-Day Encounters with Monsters of New Urban Legend and Ancient Lore.* Tarcher/Perigree.

Guiley, R. E. and Imbrogno, P. (2011). *The Vengeful Djinn: Unveiling the Hidden Agenda of Genies.* Llewellyn Publications.

Harpur, P. (1994). *Daimonic reality: A Field Guide to the Otherworld.* Viking Arkana.

Keel, J. (1975). *The Mothman Prophecies.* Saturday Review Press and E. P. Dutton.

Kelleher, C. & Knapp, G. (2005). *Hunt for the Skinwalker: Science Confronts the Unexplained at a Remote Ranch in Utah.* Paraview Pocket Books.

Lebling, R. (2014). *Legends of the Fire Spirits: Jinns and Genies from Arabia to Zanzibar.* I.B. Tauris.

Van Paassen, P. (1946). *Days of our Years.* Dial Press. (P. 248–251).

Magic and Parapsychology

Artisson, Robin. (2014). *Letters from the Devil's Forest: An Anthology of Writings on Traditional Witchcraft, Spiritual Ecology and Provenance Traditionalism.* CreateSpace Independent Publishing Platform.

Ashcroft-Nowicki, D. & Brennan, J. H. (2001) *Magical Use of Thought Forms*. Llewelyn Publications.

Belanger, M. (2021). *The Dictionary of Demons: Expanded & Revised: Names of the Damned*. Llewellyn Publications.

Carter, C. (2012). *Science and Psychic Phenomena*. Inner Traditions.

Fortune, D. (1930). *Psychic Self-Defence*. Rider & Company.

Fortune, D. (1926) *The Secrets of Dr. Taverner*. Noel Douglas.

Greer, J. M. (2001). *Monsters: An Investigator's Guide to Magical Beings*. Llewellyn Worldwide.

Miles, C., & Ramsden, H. (1907). *Experiments in Thought-Transference. Journal of the Society for Psychical Research.* /13/, 243–262.

Internet Sources

Great Dane Breed Information. (N.d.). *American Kennel Club.* https://www.akc.org/dog-breeds/great-dane/

Mastiff Dog Breed Information. (N.d.). *American Kennel Club.* https://www.akc.org/dog-breeds/mastiff

Newfoundland Dog Breed Information. (N.d.). *American Kennel Club.* https://www.akc.org/dog-breeds/newfoundland/

Ozark Howler the Hellhound. (2016). *Ozark Howler Info.* http://ozarkhowler.info/index.php/2018/12/26/ozark-howler-the-hellhound/

Bizarre Creature Encounter in Adams County, Pennsylvania. (2019, March 20). *Phantoms and Monsters: Pulse of the Paranormal.* https://www.phantomsandmonsters.com/search?q=New+Oxford

Large White Cryptid Canine / Hellhounds in Jasper, Alabama. (2019, May 02). *Phantoms and Monsters: Pulse of the Paranormal.* https://www.phantomsandmonsters.com/search?q=Jasper%2C+Alabama

Texas "Hellhound". (2018, April 12). *Phantoms and Monsters:*

Pulse of the Paranormal. https://www.phantomsandmonsters.com/search?q=Texas+Hellhound+

The Demon Dog of Valle Crucis. (2011, October 11). *Phantoms and Monsters: Pulse of the Paranormal*. https://www.phantomsandmonsters.com/2011/10/demon-dog-of-valle-crucis.html

Shuckland. (N.D.) *Shuckland*. *https://www.hiddenea.com/shuckland/introduction.htm*

Animism. (N.D.). *Wikipedia*. https://en.wikipedia.org/wiki/Animism

Black Shuck. (N.D.) Wikipedia. https://en.wikipedia.org/wiki/Black_Shuck

Chime Hours. (N.D.). *Wikipedia*. https://en.wikipedia.org/wiki/Chime_hours

Familiar. (N.D.) *Wikipedia*. https://en.wikipedia.org/wiki/Familiar

Goethe's Faust. (N.D.) *Wikipedia*. https://en.wikipedia.org/wiki/Goethe%27s_Faust

Belanger, M. (2010). Demons, Evil, and Dark Paths. *Youtube*. https://www.youtube.com/watch?v=cI7mNpYwW28

Briggs, S. (2017, March 12). Weird Norfolk: Black Shuck sighting at Gorleston, April 1972. *Eastern Daily Press*. https://www.edp24.co.uk/news/weird-norfolk-black-shuck-sighting-at-gorleston-april-1024534

Briggs, S. And Conner, S. (2019, December 7) WEIRD NORFOLK: Black Shuck's terrifying appearance in Rocklands is enough to give you nightmares. *Eastern Daily Press*. https://www.edp24.co.uk/news/weird-norfolk-black-shuck-rocklands-folklore-1485012

Briggs, S. And Conner, S. (2020, June 21) WEIRD NORFOLK: Black Shuck prowling in Blakeney – have you seen the devil dog? *Eastern Daily Press*. https://www.edp24.co.uk/news/weird-norfolk-blakeney-black-shuck-folklore-1559438

Burchell, S. (2008). *Phantom Black Dogs in PreHispanic Mexico.* https://www.hoap.co.uk/pbdpm.pdf

Draper, E. (2008). Neopaganism Growing Quickly. *The Denver Post.* https://www.denverpost.com/2008/06/25/neopaganism-growing-quickly/

Dykens, M. & Gillette, L. (N.D.) Dire Wolves. *San Diego Natural History Museum.* https://www.sdnhm.org/exhibitions/fossil-mysteries/fossil-field-guide-a-z/dire-wolf/

Field, T. Et al. (2010). Tai Chi/ Yoga Effects on Anxiety, Heartrate, EEG and Math Computations. *US National Library of Medicine, National Institutes of Health.* https://www.ncbi.nlm.nih.gov/pmc/articles/PMC2950830/

Hanley, S. (2005). *The Black Dog Mystery.* /http://www.blackdoginstitute.org.au/media/eventscal/index.cfm

Henri, S. (2017, February 7). Go Searching for the Black Dog of the Hanging Hills. *Connecticut Weekender.* https://ctweekender.com/the-black-dog-of-the-hanging-hills/

Jacobs, R. (2019, October 29). Icelanders Still Believe in Invisible Elves. *The Atlantic.* https://www.theatlantic.com/international/archive/2013/10/why-so-many-icelanders-still-believe-in-invisible-elves/280783/

Mark, J. (2016, July 25). Anubis. *World History Encyclopedia.* https://www.worldhistory.org/Anubis/

Redfern, N. (2018). Phantom Hounds of the Woods. *The Unexplained Mysteries.* http://theunexplainedmysteries.com/2018/03/25/phantom/

Rettner, R. (2015). 1 in 20 People has Hallucinated. *Live Science.* https://www.livescience.com/50999-hallucinations-delusions-common.html

Rincon, P. (2020, October 19) Dogs are humans' oldest companions, DNA shows. *BBC News.* https://www.bbc.com/news/science-environment-54690458

Swancer, Brent. (2019). *The Mysterious Demon Dog of North*

Carolina. Mysterious Universe. https://mysteriousuniverse.org/2019/02/the-mysterious-demon-dog-of-north-carolina/

Trubshaw, B. (2004). Black dogs in folklore. *At the Edge magazine Web site.* http://www.indigogroup.co.uk/edge/bdogfl.htm

Villines, Z. (2019, November 15). What To Know About Hallucinations. *Medical News Today.* https://www.medicalnewstoday.com/articles/327014

Referenced Television Shows

"Devil Dogs." *Monsters and Mysteries in America,* directed by Jean Guy Bureau. M2 Pictures, 2015.

"Hell Hound." *Monsters and Mysteries in America,* directed by Christian Faber. M2 Pictures, 2014.

ABOUT THE AUTHOR

W T Watson is a coffee addict with an abiding love of monsters, magic, Forteana and the paranormal that infuses his fictional works. When he is not writing or reading about monsters, he can be found outdoors allowing his dogs to take him for a walk around his neighbourhood in Kitchener, Ontario.

He lives with his spouse, Stacey, in a townhome that would be jammed with books if it weren't for e-readers.

Hunting The Beast: A Novel

Made in United States
Orlando, FL
01 December 2021

11021468R00162